LOVE, COVENANT & MEANING

JONATHAN MILLS

REGENT COLLEGE PUBLISHING
Vancouver, British Columbia

This edition published 2002 by Regent College Publishing
an imprint of the Regent College Bookstore
5800 University Boulevard, Vancouver, B.C. V6T 2E4 Canada
www.regentpublishing.com

The views expressed in this book are those of the author and do not necessarily represent the views of Regent College.

Unless otherwise noted, all Scripture quotations are from the New International Version of the Bible, copyright © 1973, 1978 by the International Bible Society. Used by permission of Zondervan Publishers.

National Library of Canada Cataloguing-in-Publication Data

Mills, Jonathan Peter.
        Love, covenant & meaning / Jonathan Mills.
        Includes bibliographical references.

        ISBN 1-55361-057-1 (Canada)
        ISBN 1-57383-091-7 (United States)

        1. Homosexuality — Religious aspects — Christianity 2. Sex role — Religious aspects — Christianity I. Title.

BR115 H6 M54 2002   241'.66

To Mary Bernadette
who showed us so well what it means to be brave

"Matrimony was ordained for the hallowing of the union betwixt man and woman; for the procreation of children to be brought up in the fear and nurture of the Lord; and for the mutual society, help, and comfort, that the one ought to have of the other, in both prosperity and adversity."

— *The Book of Common Prayer*

Table of Contents

Preface

Revolutions leave tons of litter in their wake: destroyed structures, dismantled traditions, confused loyalties, crippled identities. Roads in and out of the revolution are clogged with refugees dispossessed from their homes and habits, looking for a place to camp. Most of the people affected neither intended nor anticipated the change that they are now having to live with.

The sexual revolution, although long in preparation, was sudden in its happening. Sexual behavior that was common enough throughout human history but either hidden or confined to the margins, was almost overnight out in the open and vaunted. Promiscuity, adultery, pornography, sado-masochism, rape and abuse, transvestitism, homosexual practice. The kinds of sexual practice that in most civilizations and centuries were clandestine are now political causes for some, and claimed as "rights" by others.

And the Christian community is reeling, doing its best to pick up the pieces and re-fashion a moral infrastructure in our culture. A great deal of energy has gone into basic damage control. Some of our best minds have done their best to convince people of the sanity and desireability of a sexual morality that is rooted in chastity and charity. Some of our finest scholars, through careful cultural and moral studies, have exposed the outrageous and cruel lies that continue to fuel the "revolution." The issues for souls and society are enormous. Very life itself is at stake. As conditions worsen, it is understandable that some of these voices become strident. The loudest voices often end up shouting invective, railing against the conditions. But decibels don't seem to count for much in these matters.

Meanwhile, Jonathan Mills has been working away for the last several years, quietly and prayerfully, modestly and obediently, in one corner of this widespread moral devastation. He has taken hold of one aspect of the homosexual world and subjected it to intelligent and sustained consideration. His writing on the issue is a preeminent instance of the Christian mind at work; as the argument unfolds we realize how essential it is that we have friends who think Christianly, and what a difference it makes in the task of living. Dr. Mills sorts through our ethical-cultural history with immense learning, challenges the sloppiness of our diction, and dares to propose one response in the midst of the chaos that has all the marks of Gospel on it: human hope, moral integrity, God's glory.

This is bold thinking-writing-praying (the three are tightly woven into the text). But it is not impetuous. He honors the best in evangelical biblical scholarship and keeps company with trusted theological ethicists. Unlike so many of the voices that we are used to hearing on these matters, his is neither despairing nor hysterical. Faced with the massive moral disintegration of our times, we are commonly intimidated into passivity. Dr. Mills is not intimidated. He doesn't take on the entire ruined culture—he simply stakes out a modest claim and begins. But it is exactly this kind of obedient beginning that so often turns out to have large Kingdom consequences.

Eugene H. Peterson
Professor of Spiritual Theology
Regent College

Foreword

Jonathan Mills asks and responds to a question of central importance for pastoral work today. I know from my own pastoral experience that within the membership of all churches there are numerous husbands and fathers who are not "heterosexually oriented" but are what's often called "non-practising homosexuals." To me their marriages and family life appear to be neither happier nor unhappier than the marriages and family life of other men. Even those who would hesitate to recommend marriage for non-heterosexual men must surely agree with Mills that many "non-heterosexual" men will continue to marry and raise families. How are such marriages to be understood? What are we to teach about such marriages? This is an issue that is not going to go away.

Mills very sensibly observes that the sexual element of all marriages is less than what is assumed both in secular culture and in many popular Christian theologies of sexuality. He recommends that we emphasize instead the foundation of all happy marriages in love, belonging and friendship. Men who aren't "heterosexual" in the usual sense of the term can certainly fulfil this foundation of marriage as well as other men. They are also as capable as other men in the joys and challenges of fatherhood. But is Mills right to suggest that the difficulties faced by non-heterosexual men in marriage might not be so very different from the difficulties faced by heterosexual men?

We need to understand everything that is involved in such marriages — and yet such marriages cannot be understood only by surveys and studies of non-heterosexual men who leave the marriages, into which they were perhaps pressured, in order to return to homosexual relations. What about the non-heterosexual men who remain married? Is it right to assume their marriages are frauds? Is it right for Christians to back up this assumption with the authority of the biblical God? Mills powerfully confronts us with the reality that this assumption imposes upon many husbands and fathers "a heavy secret shame and fear of discovery."

One of the unavoidable difficulties with this book is that it is written from the male perspective only. Responses by women are essential if this question is to be understood adequately. But I must say Mills breaks the silence surrounding such marriages. This venture will be justified if people read his arguments with the care they deserve.

Roy D. Bell
Professor Emeritus of Family Ministries
Carey Theological College

Chapter 1

Introduction

How many, many times I have re-thought and re-written these ideas! I have tried to make this booklet as brief and accessible as possible. Pastors are so busy today, and I write this booklet for them more than for anyone else. I am indebted to several readers of various versions of the manuscript; their responses and criticisms have greatly helped me think through and clarify my main arguments.

The basic thing I want to say is that the presence of "homosexual" desires in a man does not make him incapable of marrying and raising a family. Such desires don't mean he can't fall in love with a woman. Such desires don't mean he can't be a good husband and father. Such desires don't mean he can't find marriage and family a meaningful and happy way to live. Men with such desires usually marry for the sake of love, meaning, belonging and life purpose—just as their "heterosexual" brothers usually do. Can "homosexual" desires be replaced with "heterosexual" desires? Perhaps in some cases they can. But I do not believe that "homosexual" desires must be changed before a man gains the right to marry or to continue in marriage.

By "marriage" of course I have in mind the union of woman and man. This is the meaning "marriage" has throughout this booklet. Using "heterosexual marriage" in order to distinguish the union of woman and man from "same-sex relationships" seems to me very misleading — again because such language implies that the marriage of woman and man expresses "sexuality," which means now this, now that, now something else. Besides, restricting "marriage" to the union of woman and man is congruent with gay liberationism, since "homosexual marriage" is a term rejected by gay liberationists because of its inherent "heterosexism." A belief or opinion is deemed "heterosexist" if it assumes that gay, lesbian, and bisexual relationships ought to adopt "heterosexual patterns."[1] In this way, the standards of exclusive marriage ("forsaking all others") and forbearance from I-thou degradation through sadomasochism can be said to belong to traditional "heterosexual patterns."

So I leave it to the theorists of liberation to consider whether opposition to "heterosexism" actually excuses their utter failure to provide any set of guiding principles for the adolescent whom they exhort to affirm and express his sexuality in gay relations of whatever sort. What is really going on when gay liberationism accepts as valid components of a human way of life the degradation of self and other through group sex and sadomasochistic thrills?[2] What is going on when liberationist church

---

[1] Cf. Robert Goss, *Jesus Acted Up: A Gay and Lesbian Manifesto* (Harper Collins, 1993), 226 n 45.

[2] Cf. Rev. Robert Williams, *Just as I Am: A Practical Guide to Being Out, Proud and Christian* (HarperCollins, 1992): If a sexual encounter "share[s] joy and life ... it is good and holy, even if you don't know your partner's name"; "since it is so very important in an S/M scene to pay close attention to your partner, and to communicate, often nonverbally, how it is working for each of you at any given moment, S/M sex quite often exhibits more caring and concern than many vanilla encounters" (157).

spokespersons demand church (and synagogue) ceremonies to celebrate as Divinely blessed relationships of "open monogamy" where there is no promise or implicit intention to "forsake all others"?

I don't deny that fairly strong moral hints are often given in sexuality statements and publications mailed to congregations from the denominational headquarters of various mainline Protestant churches; even if these moral hints are left implicit rather than explicitly stated, they are not therefore necessarily insincerely felt. But even when their parents are members of a liberal denomination, I dare say many children entering adolescence do not read the education packets mailed out by liberal church groups. And even among the youngsters who do read the packets, probably many of them don't fully understand the meanings that such education packets give to key terms like "affirm," "celebrate," and "society's sexual mosaic." Even if a kid understands these terms in theory, will he know how to be guided through his adolescence by them in practice? Besides, the impact on him of any implicit yet firm understandings in liberal education packets, for example, that sadomasochism is incompatible with love—however thrilling, "deeply satisfying" or "soulfully enjoyable" sadomasochism may feel—could get dissolved by other sorts of directives on sexuality in the prevailing culture. Some of these directives are even given by liberal clergy; when a noted Episcopal priest and expert on spirituality was asked whether things like sadomasochism really could be good, he replied in exasperation, "Can we stop categorizing sex, moralizing about it ...? Can we ask, 'is sex, any kind of sex, deeply satisfying? Is it soulfully enjoyable ...?' So forget about right or wrong, they don't pertain."[3] (This was said in a magazine on the Internet, something to which youngsters have far more access than they do to mainline seminaries.)

Notwithstanding, I have tried to avoid controversy as far as possible. On this issue, I make my stand on common sense, experience, and reason, rather than on Scripture. Don't misunderstand me! I don't deny that the biblical passages that seem to forbid homosexual behavior do forbid homosexual behavior — or, as I prefer to say "venery between men." I think, however, I can make my basic arguments without appealing to biblical authority. Appealing to biblical authority could make my arguments seem to be possible only on the basis of "conservative presuppositions" or even a "homophobic hermeneutic." But my point is that marriage and family make as much sense for "homosexual" men as for "heterosexual" men. As I will attempt to show, no culture before our self-destructing one thought that marriage was an "expression of heterosexuality." Our culture has gradually drifted into the opinion that marriage is an expression of heterosexuality, and our culture has gradually drifted further into teaching that "homosexual" men must be excluded from marriage. To my knowledge, no one has ever tried to think through what this massive exclusion means for men who have venereal desires toward men and for the women who marry these men (who probably make as good and as bad husbands and fathers as their "heterosexual" brothers do).

In my view, no one should be surprised that many men with "homosexual" desires go ahead and marry anyway, overriding the belief that the presence of such desires denies them the right to marry the woman they love

---

[3] Thomas Moore, quoted in Jeffrey Satinover, *Homosexuality and the Politics of Truth* (Baker Books, 1996), 242.

and to raise a family with her. They bravely venture forward despite prevailing cultural beliefs — each wondering if he is the only one with such desires who is doing so, each fearing that he violates the laws of basic honesty when he gains love and belonging through marriage without the "sexuality" that, in the opinion prevailing today, gives a man the right to such things. Yes, marriage is a troubled institution today, but marriage has always been a troubled institution. And marriage is still the best thing going for men as they try to find how to live their lives. Men who for whatever reasons are prevented from marrying have a difficult task ahead of them in finding a way of bringing meaning and order to their lives. Many unmarried men even find it difficult to get their act together at all, and remain in a state of social and personal paralysis. Every study I'm aware of indicates that married men are much healthier both mentally and physically than unmarried men. So no one should be surprised that many "homosexual" men get married despite the prohibition confronting them in our culture's opinion that only "heterosexual" men may marry and raise a family.

Chapter 2

Does "Sexuality" Mean Everything? Does "Sexuality" Mean Anything ?

I t is my hope that this book will prompt its readers to re-think what they mean by "sexuality." I take issue with almost every opinion connected with this term. I believe we need to see the things of "sexuality" in an entirely new way, in an entirely new light.

Despite the Bible's doctrines on marriage, a re-thinking of "sexuality" is necessary also for conservative Christians engaged in pastoral counseling — not because we are beset by "denial" about sex and still balk at admitting that sex is part of God's design, but because we use the term "sexuality" in completely incoherent ways. Sometimes we're utterly cynical and emphasize the "fallenness" of all human sexuality. But the next minute we're "celebrating" sexuality as though the Fall had never happened, and we talk as though we still experience our sexuality as one of God's most wonderful, happiness-bringing, and inherently meaning-laden "gifts" to us. Sometimes we adopt the tone and language of secularist anthropology and neuro-chemistry, and define "sexuality" as a way of "maintaining the human pair-bond" (i.e., keeping the male attached to the female). And then we turn to a discussion of "human sexuality" in love poems, as though the sonnets

Shakespeare wrote while thinking of his various mistresses were a response to "stimuli" from the chemical "pheromones" that wafted over to him from his wife's endocrine system. Since "sexuality" has come to mean so many things, it probably no longer really means anything at all.

No doubt someone will think to defend such incoherence by exclaiming: "All this and far more is the wonderful mystery of human sexuality, which God calls us to live out in joy, faith, and responsibleness as we struggle to express this gift with integrity and genuine freedom in an all too fallen world." How helpful are such clichés? I think such emptiness is actually wrong, since sound pastoral counseling requires clear thinking and direct communication. Fine-sounding phrases that guide people into false understandings of themselves and others can cause grave harm.

Our "celebrations" of "human sexuality" tell people that they ought to be able to proceed toward an erotic passion similar to that in Adam and Eve when they first beheld and cleaved to each other in the Garden. Yes, it is said or implied in such counseling that a man must use the "gift of sexuality" well and rightly, just as with any other gift from God, such as musical talent, intelligence, or ability in sports. But I suggest that no man really experiences "sexuality" as a wonderful gift like musical ability. There are no 12-Step groups for Music Addicts Anonymous. Yet many "theologies of sexuality" burden people with the belief that when most people, certainly all normal people, consider the "sexuality" in them, they find themselves reflecting on a wonderful giftedness like remarkable eye-hand coordination.

This prompts me to conclude that if I'm a normal person and if I have the right sort of prayer life, it should be possible for me to bring my sexuality around to the point where it is a wonderful gift just like others' sexuality.

Does Sexuality Mean Everything?

If I say that "sexuality" as a "wonderful gift" doesn't seem to be happening for me, then it's as though I'm criticizing God's creation of us male and female. But I am talking only about sexuality as it is experienced after the Fall. If someone wishes to try to imagine how life was in the Garden of Eden before the Fall, that's fine — as long as such imaginings aren't passed off as somehow still true in our fallen state. I'm sure that attempting to "mortify" our sexuality would only make things worse, but this means that our "sexuality" is something to be patiently lived with as best we can, as we await our bodies' glorious spiritual clothing in the resurrection. But it is moronic to propose to "celebrate" what we call our "sexuality" as we experience it in ourselves and others, even if only as the basis for marriage and family life.

My main objection to all our "celebrations" of sexuality is that they weigh down almost entirely against "homosexual" men. If I mention quietly to my pastor that I still feel strongly attracted to women other than my wife, probably he'll reassure me that this is to be expected "because sin lives on in us all." But if I mention to my pastor that I feel strongly attracted to men, I probably won't get such acceptance. If my pastor is a conservative, he'll probably treat this as alarming news. I must make renewed efforts in prayer until I find within myself enough "genuine sexual attraction" toward women (even if not toward my wife!) in order for me to have the right to be married. So I am not likely to mention again my struggles with homosexual desires. I may even tell my pastor some time later that the homosexual feelings have mostly gone away, even though they probably haven't.

On the other hand, if my pastor is a liberal or if I go to a secular therapist, I'll be told that I must accept my true identity. I must admit to everyone that my marriage has always been a meaningless fraud, even if it's humanly understandable that self-loathing of my true identity drove me into it. I must divorce my wife right away and begin to explore "who I really am" in sexual relations with men. Do I love my wife? Do I feel happy to be living with her as my best friend and life companion as we raise our family? Those feelings are mistaken. The feelings that have to be the foundation for my identity are my sexual desires toward men. Does she still wish our household of love and friendship to continue? It's understandable that she might feel this way, but she doesn't know what she's talking about. I'm told that I know better than she what she really wants. I'm told that I must decide that it "wouldn't be fair" to her if I were to continue on in our life together as spouses and parents of our children. If she loves me and wants our friendship and partnership to continue despite my "orientation," she simply doesn't know her true good. It is my duty to decide this for her, in my obedience to how my sexuality calls me to live.

In contrast, if my sexual desires for people other than my wife are for other women, both liberal and conservative pastors would reassure me that such desires are normal. The point is that I should pray for the strength not to act on such desires and instead continue to put my life energy into my marriage, family life, and other friendships.

Today, the "homosexual" man who wishes to remain a good husband and father must make do without such good advice. He must realize all on his own that he should pray for the strength not to act on such desires and instead continue to put his life energy into his marriage, family life, and other friendships. Perhaps he even fears to admit to God that he has sexual desires toward men, since maybe God too will tell him that his marriage and family life are invalid.

If he thinks God is a liberal, then he'll be told he must leave his wife in order to be who he is—and in order to be "truly fair" to his wife. If he thinks God is a conservative, then he'll suppose he must pray harder to transform his adulterous sexual desires toward men into adulterous sexual desires toward women — at which point even liberals would grudgingly concede that he has gained the right to remain married. Liberals maintain that successful "orientation change" is very rare, and wrong to attempt to begin with, since homosexuality is worth "celebrating" every bit as much as heterosexuality is.

Chapter 3

Marriage as Covenant, or Marriage as "Sexuality"?

As the reader can suppose, I take issue with the entire line of wishful thinking that tries to come up with a Christian understanding of "human sexuality" that can function as an enriching add-on to modern neurochemistry and psychotherapy. I am especially concerned that all such wishful thinking — both secular and believing, both conservative and liberal or liberationist — ends up teaching that "homosexual" men must be excluded from marriage.

If we look back a very short time, hardly more than a century, we do not find any use of the term "sexuality" — by Christians or by anyone else.[1] The Bible contains

---

[1] *The Compact Oxford English Dictionary* (Clarendon Press, 1991) yields the following information:

The Latin *sexus* — which refers to the distinction of male and female and probably derives from *secare* (to cut, divide) — first shows up in written English in 1382, when Wycliffe uses "sex" for the duality of animals when translating Gen 6:19. This usage corresponds to the development of similar terms from *sexus* in French, Italian, Spanish, and Portuguese at about the same time. But "sex" in the sense of venery (as in "to have sex") does
Continued . . .

love songs, love stories, teachings on marriage, and rules for sex (venery), but it doesn't interpret these things as what is today called "sexuality." The Bible contains no Hebrew or Greek word that could be translated by "sexuality." Neither is there a word in Luther or Calvin or the Council of Trent that could be translated by it.

Yet "the biblical understanding of sexuality" is now a commonplace in our discourse. Yes, you can argue that the Bible contains an implicit doctrine of "sexuality." But when a new guiding concept is introduced into our reading of Scripture the danger is that we'll interpret Scripture in light of the new concept, rather than the new concept in light of Scripture. And grave mistakes can result. The grave mistake that we are concerned with here is the belief that marriage is an "expression" of "sexuality" or "heterosexuality."

What is wrong with the theory that marriage is an expression of sexuality? This theory would be harmless if "sexuality" were taken to mean merely the division of man into male and female "sexes" and their coming together as husband and wife for the sake of procreation. But "sexuality" today almost never means the procreation

---

not show up in English until 1929 (in a work by D.H. Lawrence). "Sexual" used for the distinction between male and female appears in 1651, but "sexual" to describe human behavior does not appear until 1888 (in a reference to "sexual morality"). "Sexuality" as the distinction between male and female appears in 1800, but "sexuality" for human behavior and feelings does not appear until 1879 (in a medical text).

The words and conceptuality for hetero- and homosexuality are all very recent: "heterosexual" and "homosexual" as adjectives—1892; "heterosexual" as noun—1920; "homosexual" as noun—1912; "heterosexuality"—1900; "homosexuality"—1892. In German, these words appeared somewhat earlier, in medicine and psychiatry.

of the human species by the coming together of the sexes. Today "sexuality" almost always means first of all the totality of your desires for what used to be called "venery" — from the Latin *venerea*, meaning the things of Venus.[2] But "sexuality" now means such desires as "expressed" somehow throughout your personality, for example, in artistic sensibility, in spirituality, and in close same-sex friendships.[3] So today, everybody is taken to have a "sexual identity." And even religious and moral conservatives come to interpret marriage as "who the spouses are as sexual beings."

Common sense and everyday experience, however, show us that marriage cannot really be an "expression of (hetero)sexuality." I do not deny that marriage usually involves venery and the procreation of children. What I mean is that heterosexualness in a man is much more likely to *dissolve* his marriage than to bind him to his wife. I speak here of especially of what is called "heterosexuality" in men, but it seems somewhat true of "heterosexuality" in women too. Far from being *built up* as the spouses' venereal self-expression, marriage is first of all the *restraint* of both spouses' venereal desires — even when both spouses are "heterosexual." *Their identity as married*

---

[2] Cf. C.S. Lewis, *The Four Loves* (Collins, 1963), 85. Since the prevailing term for venereal disease is now "sexually transmitted disease" or "STD," "venereal" seems useable in its original and broader sense: what pertains to or involves Venus. Cf. the Greek "aphrodisia" (the things of Aphrodite), e.g., Aristotle, *Nicomachean Ethics* 1152b17f.

[3] Troy Perry quotes from an article in a lesbian activism journal, "If you are a woman who loves another woman you are a lesbian" (*Don't Be Afraid Anymore: The Story of Reverend Troy Perry and the Metropolitan Community Churches*, with Thomas L.P. Swicegood [St Martin's Press, 1990], 191).

is not an erotic identity but an identity in covenant and intentional purposes (belonging, friendship, raising a family).

For the sake of these purposes, a man's venereal desires are primarily *restrained,* not primarily *expressed*—even when he is primarily "heterosexually oriented." These goals elevate his life from aimless individualism into a higher purposiveness, and thus we can say that marriage is rightly a blessed or happy state. People who aren't married and raising children must find other concerns to bring high purpose to their lives. But the blessedness of marriage has never meant, and cannot mean today, "sexual fulfilment" or satisfaction in venery. It has meant and must still mean self-restraint as regards venery—a humanly beneficial and ennobling self-restraint.

Seeking venereal fulfilment always brings a reduction of high purpose. I do not try to say that the appeal of such fulfilment does not call out to us very powerfully in words and phrases like "garden of pleasures." The images of beautiful young people all around us in advertisements beckon to us as to a garden of delight. But the word "marriage" doesn't beckon to us this way. Even "polygamy" connotes not sensual delight but complex household arrangements, probably including even communal strife and jealousies.

Most "heterosexual" men have enough common sense in their hearts to laugh off any notion that marriage should be an Eden of venereal bliss. They look to marriage for purpose and belonging, and if they have good sense they settle down to learning to live with their wives in life partnership. Perhaps a decade or more ago, some "heterosexual" men and even some "heterosexual" women abandoned their spouses, using the justification that everybody has the right to a marriage that is routinely "sexually fulfilling" (venereally thrilling). A marriage that had become "sexually boring" was rightly forsaken, especially when attending various sexuality *workshops* and *seminars* did not enable the spouses to labor and study themselves back into the garden of sensual excitement. Today even though the quest for venereal fulfilment (thrills) probably contributes to divorce as much as it has always done, "heterosexual" men no longer appeal to the "right to sexual fulfilment" as a justification for abandoning their life partners.

Chapter 4

Marriage as a Covenant for which "Homosexuals" Are Deemed Unqualified

So everyone expects "heterosexual" men to have the good sense to shrug off the "celebration" of marriage as the "expression of sexuality." Indeed, I have never seen a genuinely theological treatment of marriage that considers it an "expression of sexuality" rather than a covenant formed for the sake love and friendship and belonging and partnership in raising a family.[1] Nevertheless, "homosexual" men are expected to consider marriage an "expression of sexuality" and to believe that they cannot marry or remain married in good faith. Their "sexual identity" isn't "oriented" the right way, since they would find venery with attractive men in general more thrilling than venery with attractive women in general. Since they would find venery with a variety of men more thrilling than venery with a variety of women, they must somehow realize that a covenant of love and friendship with a woman would be meaningless to them.

---

[1] On the covenantal theology of marriage, see Max Stackhouse, *Covenant and Commitments: Faith, Family and Economic Life* (Louisville KY: Westminster John Knox Press, 1997).

Here, the basic belief held by conservative Christians is the same as that held by gay liberationists: "homosexuals" (men whose desires for venery are focused mostly or entirely on men) have no *capacity* for marriage. On the one hand, liberationism teaches that homosexuals must express their "sexual orientation" in relationships of venery with men. According to this opinion, only fear, hypocrisy and denial could induce a homosexual man to suppose marrying a woman he loves and raising a family with her could be a fulfilling way of life for him. Religiomoral conservatives, on the other hand, teach that a homosexual must consider his "sexual orientation" a calling from God to a life of celibacy — unless, of course, he finds some way to "re-orient" his desires for venery away from all attractive men and toward all attractive women.

In this way, liberalism and conservatism conspire to deprive men with strong "homosexual" desires of the right to marriage and family. When a man resists strong venereal desire for someone (male or female) in order to remain faithful to his wife (whom he may find, even if he is entirely "heterosexual," no longer venereally attractive to him), his commitment to his marriage does not "express" his sexuality but the complete overriding of it. Yet the universal Christian opinion seems now to be that only the man whose venereal desires are focused mostly on attractive women in general — and who therefore must restrain his "sexuality" if he's going to be even serially monogamous — has the right to "express his sexuality" by marrying a woman he loves and raising a family with her! I suggest this entire approach makes no sense.

Chapter 5

Thoughtlessly Applying the Pressure of Biblical Authority

Conservative Christians, I think correctly, maintain that the gay liberationist argument is directly opposed by Holy Scripture. Jack Miles, a Hebrew Bible scholar who is certainly not seeking to vindicate traditional Jewish or Christian doctrine, is able to remark, "it is only by a forced political correctness that the Bible as a whole can be read as neutral on the subject of homosexuality."[1] Actually, a short while ago Christian gay liberationists held so too, but argued in the classical liberal mode that Scripture should not be adhered to as inerrant. The old-fashioned liberal argument held that if the Bible everywhere assumes the marriage of woman and man, and speaks against homosexual relations here and there, this really doesn't matter much, because the biblical authors had no understanding of sexuality as we know it today. The Bible's basic message is that God cares for us and is concerned only that we be responsible and caring in our sexual relationships of whatever sort.

Some gay liberationists still speak in the liberal mode, but they are becoming fewer as each day passes. Most

---

[1] Jack Miles, *God: A Biography* (Random House, 1995), 57.

Christian liberationists have returned to a sort of inerrancy, even if only on the passages pertinent to homosexuality. Rather than arguing that Scripture is a time-bound document that contains numerous misunderstandings, the new liberationism argues that careful exegesis proves Scripture to forbid only homosexual relations involving, for example, exploitation or cultic prostitution.[2] No longer does liberationism assert that the Bible isn't authoritative when it forbids homosexual relations; liberationism now maintains that the Bible doesn't forbid homosexual relations though it is rightly treated as divinely authoritative on such matters.

Liberationists suppose this quasi-inerrantist procedure is preferable to classic, old-fashioned liberalism with its Enlightenment mindset of rationality, progress and individualism. Yet liberationist inerrancy amounts to saying, "If the Bible did forbid homosexual relationships, I would obediently oppose them, too. Fortunately, however, the Bible doesn't forbid homosexual relationships but only such things as cultic prostitution. When we add in God's affirmation of God's creation (which includes sexuality), we can both uphold the authority of the Bible on all things and arrive at the celebration of homosexual relations on a biblical basis." But in such liberationist inerrancy, the authority of the Bible is made clear and distinct, whereas very unclear and indistinct are the arguments that the Bible forbids only homosexual relationships when they are

---

[2] Troy Perry takes a classical liberal approach to the Bible in *The Lord is My Shepherd and He Knows I'm Gay*, as told to Charles L. Lucas (Bantam Books, 1972, 1978), 137ff. Twenty-eight years later, however, he takes up the liberationist inerrancy approach in *Don't Be Afraid Anymore*, 339ff.

wrong on other grounds (e.g., their involvement in the worship of other gods or idolatry[3]).

The uncertainty of the new liberationist inerrancy approach is accentuated for "homosexually oriented" Christians when liberationist interpretations of the pertinent biblical passages differ widely from one scholar to another, so that what St. Paul opposes at 1 Cor. 6:9 is not homosexual behavior as such but definitely only cultic sexual practices, or definitely only sexual practices involving the exploitation of a youngster, or definitely only sexual practices involving prostitution, or perhaps definitely only sexual practices involving something else. This means the new inerrantist liberationism clearly re-asserts the authority of the Bible, but the affirmation of homosexual relations we're all now obligated to see in the Bible is left very unclear. So, what comes through to "homosexually oriented" men and adolescents who take the Bible seriously is that the Bible ought to be taken seriously and that the Bible may indeed forbid homosexual relations as such. No liberationist should be surprised that many "homosexually oriented" men decide to stay on the safe side of things rather than act in obedience to one or more of the various liberationist inerrantist interpretations.

The new biblically-based liberationism, then, reinforces the tendency of any "homosexual" man or youth to fear that he would violate biblical authority if he acted on his homosexual desires. It seems to me that only liberal Chris-

---

[3] The liberationist may suppose this position is easier to defend in present-day culture, but I suggest postmodernist trends are already beginning to indicate a return to "cultic prostitution," wherein certain kinds of "sexual shamans" will offer their services to the individual as ways of mediating between him or her and the co-present spirit world. Perhaps liberals will soon begin teaching that the Bible forbids only *uncaring* cultic prostitution.

tians (who also accept "inclusivized God-talk," for example) are satisfied with the new liberationist interpretations of the biblical passages pertinent to homosexuality. But liberal homosexual Christians aren't looking to have their homosexual behavior validated by inerrantist methods to begin with!

At the same time, conservative Christianity—quite without a single Scriptural passage to support its case—somehow implies that according to the Bible men with homosexual desires must refrain from marriage until their "orientation" is changed by prayer or whatever else. With liberationist and conservative understandings of the Bible bearing down on them this way, men with homosexual desires who take the Bible seriously are forced into a desolate place indeed.

Chapter 6

Are Humans Sexual Beings or Choosing Beings?

Conservative Christians should wake up to how similar the gay liberationist argument is to their belief that marriage is a relationship "expressing who the spouses are as sexual beings." This belief puts great pressure upon churches to validate "same-sex" relationships. If all of us are "sexual beings" and "sexual persons," but if some of us are (unchangeably) "homosexual persons," then how can conservative Christianity demand that these men and women refrain from expressing their being and their human personhood ? Once a man is defined as a "sexual being," it becomes a violation of his humanness and his personhood to argue that a homosexual must not express "who he is."[1]

---

[1] Conservative Protestants also fall into this difficulty, but the difficulty is made especially clear by Roman Catholic authority, which always places a high premium on clarity and definition. *The Catechism of the Catholic Church* (1994) teaches on the one hand that everybody is called to the "integration of sexuality within the person and thus the inner unity of man is his bodily and spiritual being" (¶2337). On the other hand, the catechism *Continued* . . .

These problems are not involved in the traditional Judeo-Christian view. The traditional view taught that venery should be kept within marriage, but it did not teach that marriage was the expression of the desire for venery, still less that men with venereal desires toward men had a defective kind of human personhood. In order to vindicate the traditional Judeo-Christian and indeed common sense view, I think we must argue that in light of the Scriptures, the human being is not a *sexual* being but a choosing being. Our *choices*— for good or evil — with what is given to us *are what we are* before God. Our choices ex-

---

refers to "homosexual persons" or to men and women "who experience an exclusive or predominant sexual attraction toward persons of the same sex" and thus toward sexual acts that "do not proceed from a genuine affective and sexual complementarity" (¶¶ 2357, 2359).

Roman Catholic authority does not of course intend to teach that there is something defective about the humanness or the personhood of "homosexual persons," but — as I will argue further on — it is led like present-day conservative Protestantism into this implication by its essentially Rousseauan notion of "sexuality." This Rousseauanism is expressed most clearly when the catechism maintains, "Sexuality affects all aspects of the human person in the unity of his body and soul. It especially concerns affectivity, the capacity to love and to procreate, and in a more general way the aptitude for forming bonds of communion with others. Everyone, man and woman, should acknowledge and accept his sexual identity" (¶¶ 2332f). Yet if human beings are sexual beings in this sense, and if some people are unchangeably "homosexual," and if homosexual behavior is wrong, then homosexuals are humanly and spiritually defective in some way — for example, in "genuine affectivity" — that heterosexuals are not. Clearly, Roman Catholic authority wishes not to imply this. Therefore, it should reject its Rousseauan notion of humans as "sexual beings."

press who we are as human beings since every human action (including any action involving "sexuality") requires a choice.[2] Our actions are evaluated morally and spiritually with a view to the choices that determine them. This is as true of our marriages as of anything else we do.[3]

Yes, choices involve things in our souls and bodies that are simply "given" to us (things we did not choose and for which we aren't held responsible), and you can say that when I make a choice involving sexualness or venereal desire the choice "expresses my sexuality." But it is the choice, not the sexuality, that "expresses who I am." If choice is the principle of genuinely human action, *our sexuality does not express who we are as human beings or persons.* This puts my argument at odds with every medical, psychological, or sociological method for defining human beings' "identities" in terms of their "sexual responses" to whatever "stimuli." These theories do not address but only ignore the question of choice, and I maintain this evasion amounts to confirmation of my thesis that anybody's identity as a human being can be defined only by considering how he or she chooses to live.

Since marriage is built up from decisions and commitments around love and belonging, it can't be considered a "response to sexual stimuli." Therefore, marriage is not the "expression of (hetero)sexuality" but the expression of an on-going set of choices in how to live—good choices and bad choices, competent choices and incompetent choices. Yes, some marriages "express" a lot of venereal desire between the spouses, at least at the beginning.

---

[2] Postmodernist theory, however, tends toward asserting that "choice" is only a hypocritical bourgeois epitaph added on to a sexual assertion or capitulation.

[3] Choices and choosing seem inevitable as the basis for human identity even for proponents of sexual identity. Cf. Goss, 57-59.

But venereal desire is not what a marriage is, and it certainly isn't the lifeblood of a good marriage. There is no research or common sense to suggest that "homosexual" men lack what is necessary to choose to be good husbands and to raise their families well. Most men have the capacity for sexual relations both with men and with women. And even gay liberationists admit that "homosexual" men can fall in love with women.[4] So where is the evidence that "homosexual" men — or, rather, where is the evidence that men with strong desires for venery with attractive men in general (rather than with attractive women in general) don't have what it takes to be good and loving husbands and fathers?

---

[4] Cf., e.g., Perry, *Don't Be Afraid Anymore*, 15. Mel White, Stranger at the Gate (Simon & Schuster, 1994), 86. I don't wish to be unduly harsh in my remarks on Mel White's autobiography. White's candor and bravery are commendable. And very remarkable, even astonishing, are the efforts he makes to change his "sexual orientation" — though those efforts were unnecessary in light of the Bible, and though they now seem pointless to him.

Chapter 7

A Glance at Scripture on the *Problem* of Venereal Desire

Of course, the advantage of the newer conservative Christian doctrine that "(hetero)sexuality is to be celebrated within marriage" is that this doctrine does not see sinfulness in all desire for venery, as traditional Christianity often tended to do. I agree it's quite wrong to equate "sexuality" and sin. There's no call in Scripture or common sense for that equation.

Yet, as C.S. Lewis wisely observes so many places in his works, common sense shows us that venery is too much a way of foolishness for us to "celebrate" it in the tones of high worship.[1] Veneral desire is neither the highest thing in man nor the most wicked. There is no call for a return to any identification of such desire with sinfulness. But equally there is also no call for us to begin naively jumping up and down in praise of our sex drives as guides to our happiness,[2] still less that the Scriptures teach us to "celebrate" our sex drives.

Now, as regards the Song of Songs, I'd say we should remain aware of the rich tradition in Judaism and Christianity of meditation upon the Song as disclosing important

---

[1] Lewis, *The Four Loves*, 22, 57, 90-94.
[2] Contra Mel White, 52.

truths about the relationship between God and his people. Certainly there is no tradition of its use as a manual for instruction in marriage. Quite aside from any return to allegorizing the Song in exegesis, though, I think we're mistaken today when we read it as a celebration of marriage and the highest love a woman and a man can have for each other. First of all, the Song's two separated desirers aren't married (except in some of her nightmarish love-sick dreams). Moreover, there's no indication that if the two are allowed to marry they will find, after "love-sickness" (2:5; 5:8) dies away after the honeymoon, that they are well-suited as life companions and friends. It's easy to imagine such a conclusion to the Song, but it's just as easy to imagine very different endings as well. The same passion that drives them toward each other now could drive them toward others in the future.

Indeed, the Song of Songs might include awe for the power of erotic love, which can overwhelm all rational economic considerations even in an era of scarcity (8:7), rather than a praise for eros as a bestower of happiness, shalom, and other good things. A reasonable man might wish for a loving marriage, but would he really wish to fall in love like this, especially since he could fall in such love-sick love for someone other than his wife — or, if he isn't married, for someone who can't or won't marry him? A reasonable man might rather wish that such love didn't have a grip like that of death (8:6)! He might wish that its fires could be extinguished by water (8:7)! I realize that reasonableness doesn't necessarily have the right to a final verdict in how love-sick love ought to be evaluated. I daresay infinite longings have their claims too. But however much you might wish to elevate the claims of infinite longings above reason and happiness, such wishes do nothing to show that this Song is about marriage, let alone a happy one.

But even supposing this Song actually somehow teaches that the couple involved are happily married, there is no just cause to use this most obscure book in the Bible as providing a general doctrine on "sexuality in marriage" for us today. Should pastors teach that love-sick love is the only permissible doorway to marriage? Yes, probably there are Christians still today who believe that venery is something in itself evil, so some pastors might wish to have as many biblical texts as possible to prove that Scripture doesn't condemn venery. But is this obscure book really any help in teaching the validity of marital venery in God's created order? Surely there are plenty of other biblical passages to refute the belief that venery itself is evil. Besides, it really doesn't do to force a biblical text to seem to say what it really doesn't — even when such falsification seems to serve a good purpose. And the Song of Songs really must be distorted quite a bit to make it a guidebook for spouses or even a celebration of the venereal element *in marriage.*

Since the Song is attributed to a notorious collector of wives and concubines, I'd suggest its most obvious lesson as regards Christian marriage is that venereal passion is far less likely to bind husband and wife to each other than it is to dissolve their covenant through adultery or weaken their covenant through adultery of the heart. Let us also remember that the Song of Songs has absolutely nothing to say about noble qualities of soul. The description of the ideal wife in Proverbs 31, on the other hand, is silent on the sort of attributes praised to the skies in the Song of Songs, except to point out they have no real value (v. 30). Proverbs 31 surely teaches us that a "heterosexual" man's "affirmation" of his sexuality, far from being the foundation for marriage, would lead to a "heterosexual lifestyle" like Solomon's or that of his father King David. Affirmation of heterosexuality is "the way that destroys kings" (v. 3) — and surely men in lesser stations too! Surely Proverbs

31, not the Song of Songs, is the Old Testament's primary text on marriage.

In the New Testament too, venereal desire is mentioned only as a problem, never as a foundation for marriage. The Gospel sets itself to confining venereal desire to marriage (e.g., 1Cor 7:1-9), not to celebrating marriage as the "expression of (hetero)sexuality" (cf Matt. 5:28; 15:19). I don't say the Scriptures teach that venereal desire is essentially evil, only that it is problematic — not essentially important in itself, but something to be used and restrained for the sake of what is truly important. Yes, the New Testament follows the Old in strongly venerating marriage, but it also follows the Old Testament in never teaching that marriage is to be venerated as "the expression of sexuality."

Even when a New Testament doctrine might celebrate venery within marriage, it demotes the wine of marriage by the revelation of a much higher wine. Surely this is part of the meaning of the miracle at Cana in John 2:1-11. The wine of Heaven calls some to live celibately (Matt. 19:11-12) and means that venery is less important than the higher wine even within the partnership of marriage itself (1 Cor. 7:5-7). Nothing in the Old Testament or the New adds up to a "celebration" of marriage as the "expression of (hetero)sexuality."

As regards "homosexuality" in the Bible, at this point I'll note only that any man, whatever the "orientation" of his venereal desires, could love and revere the noble woman whom the king's mother recommends as a wife for her son in Proverbs 31. The mother's teaching appeals not to the son's sex drive but to his capacity for wisdom in his heart (cf Prov. 5:3-20; 6:20-35; 7:5-27; 9:13-18). In the same way, any man could understand the agapic belongingness that St. Paul sees in marriage (Eph. 5:21-33; 1 Cor. 7:33f), since agape is not mediated through eros or lust. If anything, agape brings a different spirit and meaning to venery between husband and wife. What's called "sexual orientation" today has nothing to with such esteeming or valuing.

So when a "heterosexual" man learns to appreciate the noble woman of Proverbs 31, regardless of her looks, he is *transcending* his sexuality, not *expressing* it. Jacob labored fourteen years for Rachel "beautiful in form and beautiful of face." But Leah of the "tender eyes" (Gen. 29:17) proved a much better and nobler wife. Perhaps a "homosexual" man—a man whose venereal desires are focused more on men than on women—would not have been distracted by Rachel's looks[3] and could have seen Leah's goodness and nobility from the beginning, as Jacob did not (29:30f). Biblically, the dwindling of such desire is not grounds for divorce (Mal. 2:14-16).

Even in Genesis 2, the problem of man's aloneness isn't presented as a venereal longing: God seeks an appropriate *helper* for the man, and he first looks for this helper among the animals. Yes, before the Fall there was no division between the man's desire to "cleave unto his wife" (Gen. 2:24) and his esteem for the woman as his appropriate helper. But the disarray that besets us in many ways after the Fall is all the more reason why it makes no sense to speak of the partnership and friendship between husband and wife as an expression of venereal desire.

---

[3] Cf. Bob Davies and Lori Rentzel, *Coming out of Homosexuality: New Freedom for Men and Women* (InterVarsity Press, 1993), 161f.

Chapter 8

Something about the Realities of Male Sexuality

In the biblical passages I treated, the concern is with male venereal desire, and in this booklet I too consider primarily the sexualness of male human beings — the problem gender, the chaos gender, the gender whose venereal desires are fittingly considered alongside alcoholism (Prov. 31:4-9). Because of this chaos, most men have the capacity for sexual relations both with men and with women, though usually a man is much more drawn toward venery either with men ("homosexually oriented") or with women ("heterosexually oriented"). Male homosexual desire and male heterosexual desire in their inherent anarchy are very similar and are usefully treated together, whereas male homosexuality and female homosexuality have as little in common as male heterosexuality and female heterosexuality. I do not leave women out of consideration, and I keep in mind especially the situation of women who seek marriage and family more than venereal satisfaction. But for the most part in this booklet I consider marriage and family in relation to men of whichever "orientation."

But let me speak at this point of men who are primarily "heterosexually oriented." And here I must again remind readers of a reality that politeness urges us to overlook or at least to mention as little as possible, namely that it is really only out of shame, fear of feminist censure, and tender regard for women's feelings that "hetero-sexual" men do not more directly and openly emphasize that marriage is not a celebration of their sexualness but in a way the opposite.

Everyone was reminded of this reality by the older practice of praising the husband who "does not look at another woman twice." But this practice has been silenced by a newer opinion, which goes so far as to imply that a heterosexual man ought to make the moral effort to undo the anti-monogamous "lookism" and "ageism" that — far from being natural to him in his fallen state — has been "socially constructed" into him by the consumerist culture of patriarchal capitalism. In fact, the typical "lookist" and "ageist" heterosexual male has probably actively con-sented to getting socially constructed in this way, and thus is highly guilty that his sex drives no longer respond to moral and social-justice criteria.

Both the older and the newer moral doctrines deny to heterosexual men any "affirmation" or "celebration" of their sexuality as they actually experience it. But by praising self-restraint in contending against unchangeable (lookist and ageist) heterosexual desires, the older doc-trine encouraged such self-restraint in heterosexual men. The older doctrine also did not end up producing a com-plete silence about the realities inherent in male hetero-sexuality.

Now, there is certainly no call to routinely remind women how "lookist" and "ageist" male heterosexualness is — that is, how focused male "heterosexuality" is on fe-males who are young and beautiful according to the stan-dards of whatever culture they're in. But we shouldn't let polite silence about such lust permit secular and church authorities to teach that marriage is the expression of "heterosexuality" — and therefore also that men lacking "heterosexuality" have no right to get married and raise a family. From politeness, we have permitted the belief that a (heterosexual) man experiences marriage as the celebration of his sexuality. And this belief permits the conclusion that a homosexual man must find marriage meaningless because he lacks the sexuality marriage is the celebration of. If he cannot "change his orientation" he must forgo marriage and family, and either live celibately or venture into the whatever of gay sexuality.

Should this be taught? Does marriage and family make sense for a man only when he must restrain his desires for all attractive women? Does marriage and family make no sense to a man as life purposes when he does not have to restrain his desires for all attractive women (because the greater part of his venereal desire is focused on all attractive men)?

Chapter 9

Sexualness vs.
the Heart of Man

I don't think I'm overstating male heterosexuality's fallenness. And I don't think this is a view peculiar to the Bible. The sociologist Max Weber notes a universal tendency to demote sexuality in religions that emphasize moral fraternity.[1] In any case, the fallenness of heterosexualness means such men in marriage do not "express" their sex drives. Rather, through what the Scriptures call the "heart,"[2] "heterosexual" men transcend their venereal drives for the sake of love, meaning, and belonging. The Greek moralists refer to this part of the soul as "the spirited element." In the "heart" the soul does everything except rational intellection and appetite. Heart includes, therefore, everything interesting about human beings — moral deliberation, conscience, will or choice, promising ("commitment"), awe and worship, respect and contempt, fear, courage and anger, pride and vanity,

---

[1] Max Weber, "Religious Rejections of the World and Their Directions," in *From Max Weber: Essays in Sociology* (Oxford University Press, 1958; ed. and trans., H.H. Gerth, C. Wright Mills), 323ff.
[2] Cf. C.S. Lewis, *The Abolition of Man*, ch. 1.

hope and despair, shame, love and hatred, and who knows what else.

So it is in our *heart*, not in our sexualness, that we human beings think and decide how to live—even if the decision is to indulge in venery of whatever sort. A man sees the complementarity of woman and man not through the eyes of lust but in his heart. Jacob's lust for Rachel distracted him from perceiving the virtue of Leah, a virtue to complement or complete his. It's in his heart, not through the lust of his eyes, that a man sees or learns to see the complementation of woman and man. If a man is "homosexual" or has little lust toward attractive women, this is no obstacle to his perceiving woman as his complement or helper.

So, again, I ask, if we're realistic enough to recognize that marital friendship and partnership can't really be constructed from male heterosexuality, why do we assume "homosexual" men lack the capacity for marriage? (In the first place, men and women should not "identify" themselves by the "orientation" of their venereal drives; it would be a good thing if the terms "heterosexual" and "homosexual" dropped from our Christian and secular vocabulary.) Shouldn't we at least be asking whether the transcending of venereal desire that marriage requires of a mostly or entirely "heterosexual" man who marries for the sake of love, friendship, and raising a family isn't more or less the same as the transcendence required of a man whose venereal desire is "oriented" mostly or entirely toward men but who restrains these drives, and who marries for the sake of love, friendship and raising a family? Of course, men with little venereal desire for women can't proceed toward marriage driven by such desire. For them, marriage must develop from friendship. But wouldn't it be better if all marriages developed from friendship?

Chapter 10

The Question of "Orientation Change"

Of course, excluding "homosexually oriented" men from marriage wouldn't matter if "sexual orientation" is always changeable. But is it possible for every man who lacks the "right" sort of sexualness to express (restrain) in marriage to gain the right sort of sexualness? If so, I guess it would be okay to forbid marriage to "homosexuals" until they refocus their venereal desires away from all attractive men and toward all attractive women, thereby becoming "heterosexuals." This temporary exclusion wouldn't matter (though it might not make a lot of sense) even if such re-orientation does not in fact make a subsequent marriage actually any better for him and his wife than it would have been otherwise. (Whether a non-practised "homosexual" orientation contributes to or detracts from marital happiness is—as I will argue below—a question that has not in fact been studied by Christian or secular researchers).

But if there are men whose drives for venery cannot be re-oriented from attractive men toward attractive women, then we surely must think through what we are doing when we exhort them either (if the exhorter is a conservative) to keep a life of celibacy or (if the exhorter is a liberal) to express themselves in whatever gay sexuality is doing today. Do we have good reason to demand that such men refrain from the benefits and meaningfulness of marriage and family, even when they fall in love with a woman and want to marry her? In all cultures prior to our own, and in most cultures still today, marriage is the usual life path for men, regardless of the focus of their venereal drives. That so many men should be excluded from marriage is an unprecedented demand.

Incidentally, it is of course inexcusable for a conservative spokesman to denounce homosexual behavior and also participate in it — as though perhaps the good he does by directing others away from sinful and harmful activities compensates for such hypocrisy. In his autobiography *Stranger at the Gate*, Mel White refers to several such secular and ecclesiastical hypocrites, though without "outing" anyone by name. However, a man is also gravely hypocritical if he is himself a "non-practising homosexual" who builds his life around loving and being loved by a wife, and yet supports the liberal position that pressures other similarly oriented men and adolescents away from marriage and family, directing them instead off into the whatever of gay liberationism. I don't know of any such liberals in particular, but in view of the benefits for men in marriage and family regardless of "sexual orientation" there are probably many. It is quite possible that some married non-practising homosexuals support the liberal line that homosexuals must not marry in order to dispel any suspicions about their own sexual orientation. Such liberals keep the good of marriage and family for themselves and send other men off into likely desolation.

Chapter 11

But Does Excluding a Few Homosexuals From Marriage Really Matter?

The conservative and liberationist consensus both in secular society and in the churches is that "homosexual" men are incapable of marriage. The consensus is that however well such men may function as loving husbands and fathers, this is only a façade. Yet, even if the number of men excluded from marriage by this demand is very small, these few men matter. No one has shown any reason why they have no right to the primary institution designed by God for human belonging and purposiveness. But we should be open to the possibility that this number is very large, much larger than is shown by the current methods of surveying, which assume complete honesty in men's self-reporting of "homosexual behavior" and of strong but "unpractised" venereal desires toward other men. A married man must be silent about such things if he doesn't want to imply to himself and others that his identity as husband and father is bogus. An unmarried man must be silent about such things if he doesn't want to imply that his intention to marry and raise a family is bogus.

In the past almost all men experiencing desires toward venery with men got married and raised families. Usually they completely refrained from venery with men besides. It makes sense to suppose that most such men even today get married and raise families. Despite the new belief that marriage is an expression of sexuality, marriage has not suddenly become an erotic playground for "heterosexual" men. Neither has marriage suddenly ceased to be meaningful and fulfilling for "homosexual" men. Dr. Jeffrey Satinover notes that "the vast majority of youngsters who at some point adopt homosexual practices later give them up."[1] For all anyone knows, many, or most, or perhaps even almost all of these teenagers thereby give up a venery more thrilling for them than any venery with women could be, yet they prefer the meaningfulness and love of wife and family. Don't "heterosexual" men marry in preference for the meaningfulness and love of wife and family, over continuing or initiating a life of sexual excitement with various women? Why should this basic sacrifice in marriage of sexual freedom for meaning and belonging feel or be any different for "homosexual" men than for "heterosexual" men?

The estimation that only 2.8% of the male population is "homosexual" means that 2.8% of men admit to researchers that they engaged in "homosexual behavior" at some point during the twelve months prior to being interviewed.[2] First of all, "even" this 2.8% of men—more than

---

[1] Satinover, 22. Satinover refers here to E.O. Laumann et al., *The Social Organization of Sexuality: Sexual Practices in the United States* (University of Chicago, 1994), 295.

[2] Satinover, 100. Cf. the summary of this survey in *Time* (Oct. 17, 1994), 46ff. The research team did undertake standard methods to ensure a genuinely random sampling of Americans, but only 79% agreed to be interviewed (*Time*, 54); the researchers suppose they can't do other than to assume that the other 21% would have given proportionately identical answers to the
Continued . . .

one in every 36! — shouldn't be declared incapable of marriage and family, if in fact they could become capable of building their lives around love and belonging with a woman. Moreover, this statistic says nothing about what percentage of men are actually involved in venery with men but deny it. Still larger must be the number of "nonpractising homosexuals" — that is, men who, whether married or not, refrain from venery with men but who would find it more thrilling than venery with women.

I have mentioned to various people the possibility that the proportion of "homosexually oriented" men in the population is, for the reasons I've cited above, much larger than anyone supposes. And I'm always surprised at the number of people who try to refute my reasoning by asserting vague theories of Darwinian adaptation and survival. Even Christians who are skeptical of the theory of evolution tend to suppose that men with a "homosexual orientation" are not likely to be fathers and thus would be quickly "weeded out" in a process of natural selection. But this assumes far too much about the motives required of males in our species not only to procreate but to raise their young up into competent adults. If the Cro-Magnons or whoever were human, they had souls and felt purpose and belonging in family life as much as people do today. Because of the vulnerability of human

---

rest. The research team admits that many people might have answered questions with selective honesty (*Time*, 50), but seem to hold that because interview methodology does not have a solution to this problem, readers are morally obligated to give the team a break and be "convinced ... that this sample is an excellent one from which we can make generalizations about sex in America" (*Time*, 54). The researchers themselves show some hesitation to conclude that only 2.8% of men are "homosexual" (*Time*, 50).

young in comparison with the young of other species, these factors probably were as powerful determinants in the successful parenting of little caveboys and cavegirls back then as these factors are in the successful parenting of children today. "Heterosexual desires" don't correlate with good parenting in men now, so they probably didn't back then. So we really have no reason to suppose that homosexual desires in men are likely to disappear in the course of natural selection.

Incidentally, it is impossible to estimate for yourself with any accuracy the proportion of "homosexual" men by considering the men in your social environments (taken to be representative of the population in general) and guessing at their "orientation." One of the absurd things in Mel White's autobiography is his assumption that all male adolescents and adults are "heterosexual" unless they are either "practising homosexuals" or absolutely coming apart at the seams by trying to obliterate such desires in themselves and extorting "normal" desires into themselves by will power. White draws this conclusion in the entirely unsupported belief that only a "small percentage" of people with homosexual desires can successfully restrain those desires for most of their lives.[3] He gives no reason for this assumption. In any case, whatever some may suppose, it is impossible to guess "sexual orientation" from a man's appearance.[4] If "homosexuals" were actually likely to be soft and cowardly, they'd never think to volunteer for the armed forces and there'd be no controversy over whether "homosexual behavior" is compatible with military service. Moreover, there's now research to

---

[3] Mel White, 217.
[4] Cf., e.g., Randy Shilts, *And the Band Played On: Politics, People, and the AIDS Epidemic* (St Martin's Press, 1987), 70; Perry, *Don't Be Afraid Anymore*, 238.

suggest that guys that make a big to-do about their toughness, about the sexiness of particular young women, and about the contemptibility of homosexuals, are more likely to be trying to draw attention away from certain feelings or secret encounters of their own than anything else.[5] In order to convince others and even themselves that they are "normal heterosexuals," "real men," etc., some men go so far as to seem obsessed with girl-watching or heterosexual pornography, or become prodigies of womanizing or even sexual harrassers of women. And as regards a man's "body language" or mannerisms, everyone was surprised to learn that Rock Hudson was homosexual, yet many people nevertheless keep on trying to guess the "orientation" of men in their social environments or on TV and in movies.

---

[5] Cf. the summary in Michae! Segell, "The Male Mind," *Esquire* (Feb. 1997), 35; and William H. Masters, et al, *Heterosexuality* (Harper Collins, 1994), 440.

Chapter 12

The Grave Situation of the Young "Homosexual" Teenager

It would be helpful to adolescent males contending with desires for "homosexual behavior" in themselves if the belief that a man's "orientation" can be guessed from his appearance or marital status were replaced in the public mind with an awareness that the venereal desires of almost any man past or present might—for all any outside observer knows—be focused much more on men than on women. Within conservative Christianity and many other places besides, the unthinking assumption is that every man, present or past, worth designating as a role model for young people is "a heterosexual." I'm sure many readers must feel that to assume anything else would be the height of impoliteness, especially since (by today's understanding) to suppose anything but utter "heterosexuality" in a man is an insult to him. If he is married, the implication is that his marriage (however faithful) is a fraud. If he is celibate, his celibacy (however complete) is deemed pious humbug; since only heterosexual celibacy is worth our esteem, his celibacy is thought to merit only our condescension and pity.

Readers who consider it "unnecessary" (and therefore extremely wrong) to speak of these matters at all probably consider my frankness here to be totally uncalled for. But our squeamish silence that we pass off as "politeness" leaves many a youngster with no role models at all. From the secular media he's aware of who knows what about "gay sexuality" and "homosexual orientation," but he has no idea that many men who today would be called "homosexuals by orientation" have been fathers and husbands and even saints of the church. So he has no idea how to live his life.

A critic might retort, "But historical investigation hardly ever can discover any indications of homosexuality in saints and church founders, and certainly no evidence at all if they remain perfectly celibate or faithful husbands! Why then assume any of them are this way?" But I don't suggest anyone in particular "is homosexual." What I mean is almost anyone in history could be, and there's no reason why a youngster contending with these desires in himself must restrict himself only to "homosexual role models" until he can extort an "orientation change" out of himself. Remember: he will be aware of these desires years and years before he will be old enough to think of entering therapies or ministries that promote orientation change. *Do you want him to fear that the only males like him in the world are the ones he hears about in the media?*

The cowardly conservative silence that passes itself off as "politeness" when in fact direct honesty is required leaves such a kid to suppose he must repress the part of his desire that he finds unable to change by will power and prayer. If he finds his desires unchanged, he may despair and think of suicide or begin to experiment with who knows what part of the "gay lifestyle" he happens to encounter. Conservative parents and educators won't mention even St. Augustine's venery with men[1] since they

---

[1] *Confessions* iii 1 is not a discussion of pre-marital sex with girlfriends at Carthage High. Cf. also his admission (viii 1 — where *Continued* . . .

suppose that even mentioning such realities to a youngster might "confuse" him or "give him the idea." Sure, and don't mention drugs to him, because that will only give him the idea. And don't ask a depressed kid if he's thinking of suicide, because that will only give him the idea. Or, if he must hear of homosexuals at all, let it be only in the context of warnings about AIDS—such warnings will indeed make him pray extra hard to God to change him—and if this change doesn't happen, who knows what he will conclude!

Of course, Christian liberals will tell him of "homosexually oriented" heroes like Socrates. But they won't mention that Socrates was married and had three sons, or that Socrates thought venery between men is wrong and refrained from it himself.[2] Presumably, liberals feel it would only "confuse" a youngster to remind him that almost all homosexual men before our time got married and raised families and that probably most still do so even today. Neither liberals nor conservatives ever wonder whether teaching that "homosexuals" are excluded from marriage and family life contributes to the suicidal despair that many such youngsters feel. As for whatever realities that may confront a young male who ventures off

---

he also discusses his being gripped by woman's appeal) that he had at one point in his life also fallen into the error of Rom 1:21ff. In his exegesis of Rom 1:21ff, Karl Barth speaks to male sexualness that isn't oriented essentially toward women, both in *The Epistle to the Romans* (Oxford University Press, 1968; trans., Edwyn C. Hoskyns), 51-53, and in *Church Dogmatics* (T&T Clark, 1961; trans., G.W. Bromiley), III iv 164-66. Cf. also *Church Dogmatics* IV ii 795-98.

[2] Though it contains a number of typos and oversights, cf J. Mills, "John Boswell's Corruption of the Greeks," 18:3 *Crux* (Dec. 1982), 21-27.

into gay sexuality, liberals presumably believe that the ideal of "responsibleness" and an awareness of "internalized homophobia" have the power to guide a kid safely through, no matter what older males pressure, trick or otherwise bamboozle him into "consenting" to. As in the seduction of young teenage girls by older males, the idea seems to be that if the kid "enjoyed" the encounter (experienced a thrill in it), it's utter hypocrisy for him to try to say he didn't want the encounter. Unfortunately, this line of rationalization is congruent with emerging "postmodernist" notions of self which teach that choice, consent, and individuality are mistaken bourgeois interpretations.

Let me say again that a kid should be allowed to pick out any role models he wants and assume that they were "non-practising homosexuals." He may as well, because even if the men he holds up as role models and heroes for himself did not in fact have any venereal desires toward men, whatever it is that he admires them for doing (founding churches, piloting jet aircraft, heroism under fire), it's certain that many, many other men who have done those things have been partly or completely "homosexually oriented" (practising or not).

Let's suppose he selects J.S. Bach as one of his role models. What harm is there in that? Even though certain historical facts of which the kid is unaware prove positively (let's suppose) that Bach was "100% hetero," certainly numerous musical geniuses in the past were "homosexually oriented" (practising or not), even though history (from the paucity of evidence of people's personal lives) can discover evidence of "practising homosexuality" in only a few.

Readers who feel it slanders the greatest composer of church music even to mention his name in this sordid context can now rebuke me by insisting that my disgusting attack on Bach's character, good name, and musical genius is absolutely uncalled for in view of the twenty-three children he fathered, since certainly no "homosexually oriented" man could achieve such a thing! Well, that assumption is naive, but I'll let it pass.

Chapter 13

The Institution
of Marriage

For ancient Greece and Rome, for Judaism and Christianity, and for every other culture I'm aware of except our own, marriage is primarily a household arrangement for the raising of children, not an "expression of sexuality." Societies before our own put great emphasis on procreation and the institutions that protected it. Famine, disease, and high rates of infant mortality were always about to wipe the population out entirely. Patriarchal pride put a high premium on the generation of many sons. And children were members of the family labor force ("economics" derives from the Greek word for "household"). Because of these pragmatic concerns, not because the law commanded the "expression of sexuality," the procreative element in marriage was obligatory (an old name for sexual intercourse was one's "conjugal duty"). Various punishments were prescribed for venereal deeds that threatened, or seemed to threaten, procreation and the raising of children. But that a man would experience venereal desires for people other than his wife was a matter of little importance and was assumed as a matter of course. This was true even in "Christian" societies, some of which even condoned prostitution as a "necessary" evil and frequently turned a blind eye to a certain amount of venery between men as well.

In all this, the basic societal concern (however incompetently this concern may have been expressed) was to support and protect the raising of children. There was no talk of fostering the "normal sexual development" of "the human person." Even in very strict Christian societies, though the greater part of a man's venereal desires might be focused on men, if he restrained those desires and raised a family he was in every sense a good husband, father, citizen, and Christian — not a certain type of "sexual person" who must identify himself as "a homosexual." What is today called "homosexual behavior" was forbidden, but those tempted toward such behavior were not deemed to be defective as men or somehow blind to the complementarity of woman and man in the order of creation. In medieval asceticism, the struggles of one monk to mortify his lust ("sexuality") for men did not mark him out as having a different sort of "personhood" from another who struggled to mortify his lust for women.[1] Today, everybody is pressed to socially construct himself or herself as a certain kind of "sexual person." But previously it never occurred to anyone to suggest that men with strong desires for venery with men should be excluded from marriage. Law and social convention obliged them to marry and raise children like every other man.[2]

It shocks us that in previous eras it wasn't supposed that husband and wife would likely be each other's best friend. Simple cooperation and companionability in the household economy was considered quite enough for a good marriage. The emphasis on marriage as a friendship

---

[1] Goss, 192; John Boswell, *Christianity, Social Tolerance, and Homosexuality: Gay People in Western Europe from the Beginning of the Christian Era to the Fourteenth Century* (University of Chicago, 1980), 164f.

[2] Cf. Plato, *Symposium* 192b.

is fairly recent, but this seems to me a very necessary improvement because of the incessant mobility demanded by today's economic realities. Formerly, you belonged someplace where you were rooted in an arrangement of multi-generation extended-family and neighborhood relations. But for us, community isn't secured in the routines of daily life, so it makes sense to emphasize the building of friendship between husband and wife, since economic mobility may dissolve every other relationship. I and Thou against the world.

What makes no sense is using our society's unprecedented freedom from procreative necessity to interpret marriage as an "expression of sexuality." Of course, we shouldn't concentrate on the formation of good marriages without remembering that this doesn't provide community for people who remain single. It's wrong to imply that unmarried people lead meaningless lives. But equally we shouldn't invent reasons (e.g., "homosexual orientation") to exclude people from marriage when they are actually entirely capable of it—and research, which I treat below, indicates "homosexual" men are entirely capable of being good husbands and fathers.

Because of modern medical care and food production, it is no longer necessary today to bind marriages to extreme procreative efforts. Law and public policy should still support parents in the raising of children into competent citizens and morally responsible human beings. Parenthood is still the most important social task of all. But advances in medical science and food production give us comparative freedom from procreative necessity, so it is possible even for conservative Christians to teach that marriage "expresses who we are as sexual persons." Yet not only is this view of marriage contrary to Scripture, as I've outlined briefly above. It is also humanly impossible—as much for men whose venereal desires are focused mostly on attractive women as for men whose venereal desires are focused mostly on attractive men. When a heterosexual man "expresses who he is as a sexual being," the result is never monogamous marriage but such things as adultery, serial fornication, casual venery, pornography and the hiring of prostitutes. If we are going to refer to "heterosexual monogamy" at all (and I think we shouldn't), we should emphasize that monogamy for a heterosexual man really isn't the *expression* of his sexuality, but its *subordination* to a relationship of friendship and partnership. The problem of "fear of commitment" in many heterosexual men today does not result from a lack of "genuine" sexuality in them. Such men remain thoroughly genuinely "sexual" and indeed fear marriage as a "trap" that will make them unable to celebrate their sexuality with a succession of attractive young women. They may be "immature" in heart and mind if they refuse to transcend this desire for serial monogamy. But I argue no man's heterosexualness ever matures beyond the level of such wishes.

Chapter 14

Venery and the Institution of Marriage

B ut even if marriage requires a heterosexual man to transcend his sexuality rather than to "express" it, don't we still have to hold that a man with strong desires for venery with men just doesn't have what it takes to be a good husband? No. The research I'm aware of does not show sexual passionateness is a necessary requirement for a happy marriage. Yes, some men with strong "homosexual" desires are in extremely unhappy marriages. But there is extreme unhappiness in the marriages of many "heterosexual" men too. Even when writing about women in failed marriages with men that had attempted to turn away from habitual homosexual behavior, two researchers observe,

> Many of the couples' courtships evolved from friendships. The qualities mentioned most often by the wives that they found attractive in their future husbands were: Lack of sexism, caring, sensitivity, kindness, loving, thoughtfulness, gentleness, interesting personality, exciting, adventurous and a good sense of humor. Several mentioned that they liked the fact that their future husbands desired in-

timacy more than [venery], which they did not find among other [i.e., "heterosexual"] men.[1]

Admittedly, these marriages failed, and it is devastating to be abandoned by your spouse for somebody else of whichever sex. Nevertheless, this research shows that the women did not think the absence of venereal passionateness from their husbands made them in any way inadequate as husbands. This must be even more true of husbands that do experience strong venereal desire toward men but never act upon them.

I think we must assume that the marriages that do not end in divorce because the husband begins or returns to homosexual behavior can be as happy as the marriages that do not end in divorce because the husband begins or returns to heterosexual behavior. The successful marriages of "homosexual" men can't be studied because both researchers and the spouses define such marriages as "heterosexual." I have read of no case of divorce because of a man's "homosexual orientation" where it was the wife, not the husband, who wanted out of the marriage primarily because of venereal dissatisfaction. Venery that men might consider "merely affectionate" many women find very satisfying.[2] In *every* case I've heard of where a marriage ended because of the husband's homosexual activity, the wife wished the marriage to continue if it was working well as a friendship and family partnership.

Researchers have no real idea what proportion of married men have strong venereal desires for men. Since all research depends upon honest replies to questions about

---

[1] Mary Franzen Clark and Mary Elizabeth McKheen, "When Gay Christian Men Marry Straight Christian Women," *Journal of Psychology and Christianity* 13:3 (1994), 257.
[2] Davies and Rentzel, 138-41, 154.

behavior and fantasies, many men who have them are too ashamed to admit to them—probably in many cases even to themselves or to God. The only "married homosexuals" that have come to the attention of researchers and been studied are actively homosexual men who socially construct themselves as homosexual by identifying themselves as "gay" and whose marriages fail. This means researchers actually have no idea of the happiness of marriages in which the husband experiences strong homosexual desires but remains faithful, because all observers interpret such husbands and such marriages as "heterosexual."

Andrew Greeley shows that your "feeling of importance" to your spouse "is more powerful a predictor of marital happiness" than is "sexual satisfaction" (116).[3] Admittedly, "sexual satisfaction does make a contribution of its own [to marital happiness] above and beyond that made by the spouse's ability to make the respondent feel important": "Of those who report both very great sexual satisfaction and the feeling of importance, 84% are very happily married, but even those who report importance without such a high level of sexual satisfaction, 65% say they are very happy" (116). Moreover, these statistics do not constitute proof that "homosexual orientation" in the husband precludes or even reduces "sexual satisfaction" either for the wife or the husband, especially when the spouses measure "sexual satisfaction" in terms of affection and additional importance to the other. The research involved does not attempt to distinguish sexual "satisfaction" from sexual excitement. Moreover, "*frequency* of lovemaking" has "no significant relationship"

---

[3] Andrew Greeley, *Faithful Attraction: Discovering Intimacy, Love, and Fidelity in American Marriage* (New York: Tom Doherty, 1991).

with "marital happiness" and hence also no significant relationship with sexual satisfaction (116). And the research even assumes that all participants in the study — since they are married! — are "heterosexual" (18). Some may suppose that these researchers should be faulted for not asking the study's participants "Are you a homosexual?" or "Is your husband a homosexual?" But I doubt such questions, no matter how worded, could elicit much honest data in this matter because in view of the prevailing assumption among both conservatives and liberationists that marriage is rightly an "expression of heterosexuality," answering "yes" would imply that the participant's marriage is ipso facto invalid, pointless, and a fraud.

My conclusion is that sociologists and psychologists have no reason to suppose that a good husband and father cannot be "socially constructed" equally well from a man with "homosexual" sexuality as from a man with "heterosexual" sexuality. In fact, since the research that Greeley uses shows coerced venery to be so disastrous for a marriage (98-100), it might be that heterosexualness in the husband, even if it prompts him not to force but only to pressure his wife into venery, is more likely to correlate with marital unhappiness than is homosexualness in the husband. Even Mel White won't go further than to assert that only "in most cases" a "homosexual" should not marry a "heterosexual."[4]

It is realities like these that make me conclude that in *The Four Loves* C.S. Lewis would have done well to treat venery in connection with marital Affection as well as in connection with Eros. Affectionate venery is not dependent upon passionate excitement, which is hardly likely to prevail throughout any marriage. In fact, the research

---

[4] Mel White, 213.

Greeley uses shows that the "most powerful" "correlate of marital happiness" the research discovered is whether spouses "pray often together or not" (189).

For all these reasons, I conclude that the research that exists, such as it is, supports my conclusion that "homosexual orientation" is probably no more likely than "heterosexual orientation" to correlate with marital happiness. As for parenthood, I can't think there is be any reason to suppose "homosexual orientation" detracts from fatherhood. Of course, if a man tells himself that his venereal desires toward men make his marriage and family life a fraud, this might make him depressed and thus distant and perhaps irritable as a father and a husband. But he has no reason to tell himself that. He has no reason to believe that homosexual desires compel a man to identify himself as "a homosexual" and thus as a man with no right to marriage and family.

So, after this survey of the research, again let me ask, are we—here, both conservatives and liberationists—right to assume that such a man has no capacity for the primary relationship instituted by God for human belonging? And exactly what is it in him that we're assuming makes him incapable of marriage? The presence of strong venereal desire toward attractive men? Or the lack of strong venereal desire toward attractive women—since this lack usually, though not always, occurs with the presence of strong desires for venery with men?[5] Is a woman to be shamed for entering marriage with a man whose drives for venery aren't focused on her because they are focused mostly toward attractive men? If so, this rule should be

---

[5] Troy Perry, though considering himself always "homosexual," desired venery with his wife much more than she did with him; and she was, as it seems from his account, "heterosexual" (*Don't Be Afraid Anymore*, 15, 21). Cf. also Mel White, 87, 177.

applied also to a woman who marries a heterosexual man influenced by the insane aestheticization of women's beauty in today's media. (Even averagely attractive women seem somewhat disappointing to thoroughly heterosexual men who have been incessantly bombarded by the stunningly beautiful young women on TV and in movies. If pornographic images have also been indulged in, the reduction of veneral desire within the marriage is likely to be that much greater.) If the standard that forbids marriage to "homosexual" men were consistently applied, it would forbid marriage to almost all "heterosexual" men too!

If the self-transcendence required of the "homosexual" who marries is similar to the self-transcendence required of the "heterosexual" who marries, neither Christian doctrine nor secular theories have cause to teach that marriage must be forbidden to men whose desires for venery are focused mostly or entirely on attractive men rather than on attractive women. The husband and father who restrains his desire for women other than his wife should indeed be told he is "normal" and doing the right thing with his fallen venereal desires. But the husband and father who is restraining similar desires but for men should be told the same thing. We should not weigh him down with the idea that his marriage and family life is a fraud. We should not assume he can't really feel he belongs with his wife. We should not assume he can't really find marriage and family meaningful and well worth the sacrifice of venereal freedom. His self-restraint for the sake of marriage and family is at least as great as that of any "heterosexual," but he isn't praised for it. Instead, he must fear that if the truth were known about his "sexual identity" he'd lose everyone's respect — to say nothing of the right to remain in his marriage. In no culture but ours would this conclusion be drawn about the marriages of such men. Are we really doing right and indeed speaking the Word of God when we impose this heavy secret, shame and fear of discovery upon such men?

I don't say a man with strong venereal desires toward all attractive men and relatively weak venereal desires toward women ought to marry: celibacy is right for some people, and for various reasons. External realities impose it upon some people (e.g., most widows and many divorcées) regardless of their wishes, and they must make a virtue of necessity.[6] But it is strange and I think quite wrong that conservative Protestantism, which used to repudiate the tradition of celibacy, is now assuming that celibacy is the right way of life for a large number of men as a matter of course simply because they aren't "heterosexual" — that is, because they lack the commitment-phobic lust that prompts other men toward all attractive women regardless of marriage covenants. Similarly, Roman Catholic authority, which used to teach that a special grace was required for a life of celibacy, now teaches that celibacy is the right way of life for such men as a matter of course, as though they were incapable of giving and receiving the love and friendship that many women seek from marriage far more than anything else.[7]

---

[6]Cf. Paul Dinter, "Disabled for the Kingdom: Celibacy, Scripture and Tradition" *Commonweal* (Oct. 12, 1990), 571-76.

[7] Cf. the new *Catechism of the Catholic Church* (1992), ¶¶ 2357-59. In contrast to previous Roman Catholic authority on marriage, the new catechism is completely silent on 1 Cor. 7:9; and this silence would seem to derive both from an awareness of "homosexual orientation" and from an awareness that the marital I-thou is not rightly treated as a "remedy for lust" (which is, of course, an understanding that marred traditional Protestantism too). The opinion that "homosexual" men must not marry could be thought a vestige of the notion of marriage as a remedy for (male) lust: since a "homosexually oriented" man is not likely to *Continued . . .*

use venery with his wife as a remedy for his lust, we suppose that it makes no sense for him to marry.

The impulse to be silent on 1 Cor. 7:9 in a theology of marital venery is right, since the words themselves, if taken out of the shortened eschatological horizon (cf 7:29, 31) in which St. Paul spoke them, produce an understanding of marriage that just cannot be fitting—namely, as a "remedy for lust." On the one hand, such a definition of marriage excludes from marriage men for whom venery with a woman cannot be "lustful," and would deem now defective the marriage of a man for whom venery with his wife is no longer lustful. Moreover, this definition ended up delaying the recognition in modern societies that a woman should not "have to consent" to the "conjugal act" with her husband whenever he wished. In sum, 1 Cor. 7:9 reveals the eschatological import that faith perceives in the events of daily existence, but does not provide a theology of marriage.

Of course, the right instrumental "remedy for (mere) lust" is not foisting oneself upon one's wife regardless of her wishes and counter to the meaning of marriage as an I-thou. The right remedy is self-release or "ipsation" (the term in traditional moral theology for solitary, as contrasted with mutual, masturbation). Though his understanding of the matter leaves much to be desired, St Augustine was right to forbid men to pressure their wives into venery the wives were averse to. Yet, rather than commending ipsation to the men for release, Augustine preferred on grounds of necessity to condone prostitution, with all its dehumanization and exploitation (*De Ordine* 11 iv 12; *De Bono Conjugali* 11; reference in Boswell, 149). Cf. also Thomas Aquinas, *Summa Theologica* 2-2 q154 aa11-12. (The question of ipsation's illicitness I treat below, in connection with Rousseau's attempt to channel all our sexual energy into the life blood of marriage.)

The biblical basis for a theology of marriage must be sought elsewhere, and indeed the new Roman Catholic catechism upholds Gen 2:24 and its confirmation in the Gospels (even though, in contrast to the catechism, Gen 2:24 does not speak of *Continued . . .*

Mel White would have it that if a man is drawn to glance at the handsome young male models rather than the beautiful young female models in "those full-page ads for tight-fitting jeans or underwear in newspapers and magazines," then he cannot sincerely wish "to come home after a hard day's work" to a woman who "greets him with a smile and a hug."

Such a man can be pleased only if another man greets him that way. A woman cannot "bring him comfort by her very presence," and "a woman's company" cannot "make him feel safe, comfortable, and at home."[8] Yet I submit that White's account of his own marriage shows that such a man can find friendship and meaning in life partnership with a woman and raising a family with her. What detracted from his married life was not his homosexual desires but his belief that these desires made his marriage and his faith life invalid, and the tremendous energy he

---

the "sexuality" of "the innermost being of the human person as such" [¶ 2361]). If Catholic authority does not wish to affirm the "sexuality" of those it calls "homosexual persons" (¶ 2359), but also (quite rightly) wishes to deem their "personhood" in no way defective, perhaps it should reconsider its decision to exclude so many men (and women) from Gen 2:24 (¶ 2359) simply because their "sexualness" is fallen in one way, not another. The statement "Sexuality is ordered to the conjugal love of man and woman" (¶ 2360) can be considered true only in the past tense, that is, before the fall. My arguments here apply of course to other Christian authorities making similar exclusions from the marital covenant on grounds of incapacity by "sexual orientation": I turned to this new catechism because the logic always attempted in the Roman Catholic system of doctrine is illuminating even when one must consider the system substantively mistaken in its particulars.

[8] Mel White, 261.

unfortunately thought it necessary to put into trying to re-orient his sexualness toward all attractive women.

Chapter 15

"Liberal" vs. "Conservative" and the Postmodernist Sea Change

Of course, a gay liberationist might oppose my argument in this way: "It's misleading to ask why homosexual men are assumed to be incapable of marriage, since the point is that their sexuality makes them capable of sexual relationships with men. Homosexual men wish to marry a woman and raise a family only when pressured by homophobic influences — especially conservative Christianity's wrong interpretations of the Bible and church tradition." The opinion that only a "heterosexual" would find marriage and family meaningful is very old,[1] but it is not likely to be true — unless, for example, we are to suppose that what was aroused in King David when he sees Bathsheba bathing was an insight into the complementarity of woman and man and an intention to marry and raise a family with her. This opinion is, moreover, refuted by the existence of men who, like St Augustine, experience strong venereal desires both for men and for women. Are we to

---

[1]Cf. Aristophanes in Plato's *Symposium* 192b.

declare that "bisexual" men have only a half-hearted wish for marriage and family?

There isn't space here for me to contribute to the interminable controversy surrounding Biblical exegesis on whether venery between men is forbidden really or only apparently by Torah and Gospel. My concern here is to point out that marriage and family, for all their difficulties, are still today the basic belonging to which most men aspire, and to point out that this aspiration for marriage and family isn't based in venery. Quite aside from "internalized homophobia" and the authority of Scripture and church or synagogue, there is every reason to suppose that marriage and family seem as purposeful and fulfilling (and as difficult and challenging) to most "homosexual" men as to most "heterosexual" men. I think we must assume that numerous men choose to marry and raise a family and willingly forgo "expressing" their desires for venery with men. And I think this transcendence of their venereal desires is probably not much different from the transcendence required of "heterosexual" men who choose to marry and raise a family, and willingly forgo "expressing" their drives for venery with all attractive women. The sacrifice of venereal freedom for the sake of meaning and belonging seems worth it to "homosexual" men who marry. The question is whether we ought to make their life far more difficult by teaching that it is wrong for them to marry.

The liberationist counter-argues that the solution to the shame and fear of discovery carried by married "homosexual" men is to validate gay relations among men. Yet here we confront the conflict within gay liberationism between liberalism and postmodernism. In its classic meaning, liberalism is the belief in progress for man and society through reason and scientific enlightenment. Classic liberalism accords sacred status to the conscience and to individuals in their inviolable rights and freedoms. It is a kind of secularization or this-worldly application of the Judeo-Christian understanding of the soul before God. Postmodernism, on the other hand, is emphatically and intentionally less coherent than liberalism, which it dismisses as "Enlightenment rationality." Except when elements of various postmodernist critiques are subordinated to a Judeo-Christian worldview, postmodernism guides itself through essentially negative and negating terms, such as "post-structuralism" and "deconstructionism." Personal responsibility and the moral meaning of the individual are not treated except as figments of the "capitalist metanarrative."

Although many ethicists, including Christian ones, have appropriated various elements of postmodernist critiques of technological society, there are no post-modernist ethicists in the strict sense, since ethics is the articulation of good and evil, right and wrong, by discursive reason. And this postmodernists hold to be impossible: reason is not merely value-neutral; reason is a tool for concealing or revealing power relations. According to postmodernists, reasoning's task is only to show the discontinuities in rational "metanarratives" (e.g., Christian natural law theories) for the sake of opening cultural space for the emergence or revealing of the voices that rational metanarratives are said to suppress.

While it has always been recognized that human beings are to some extent "socially constructed," postmodernism tends to consider human beings *entirely* socially constructed or formed by the "writing" of power on bodiliness.[2] Postmodernist theories show their debt to Marxism when they assail liberalism as the ideology of capitalist interests — as by asserting that individual rights are a cloak for vested interests, and that the bourgeois

---

[2]Cf. Goss, 203 n11.

"social text" must be critiqued in order to open spaces for "alternative voices." But postmodernist theories are also highly unMarxist in their willingness to deny the claim made for reason by both liberalism and Marxism, namely that reason is the privileged perspective. According to Marx, scientific analysis discloses "what must be done." But according to postmodernism, scientific analysis is as likely to become the tool of capitalist power as anything else — if indeed all science isn't essentially a class-based production of knowledge to begin with.[3] Because post-modernism has the greater analytic power — or leastwise the greater prestige — liberal ideals (humane problem-solving, scientific progress, individual rights, the ethos of personal responsibility, etc.) are increasingly discredited in technological society's leading universities and other opinion-forming institutions.

The classically liberal approach to homosexuality was to maintain that it should be legitimated and normalized by patterning its expression on middle-class "heterosexual monogamy." The basis for such monogamy is understood to be the volitional commitment of the spouses to each other as partners in the responsible tasks they decide to undertake together. It goes without saying that classical liberalism considers sado-masochism or even "open monogamy" in "gay" or "straight" partnerships to be utterly incompatible with human dignity. But this normalizing

---

[3]Postmodernism does not require rational consistency from itself but rather uses that criterion against doctrines (e.g., liberal democracy, conservative Christianity) that claim to be consistent with reason. Goss doesn't hesitate, therefore, to refrain from pressing scientific claims against conservative doctrines (e.g., 11-13, 21-23, 90-99, 194 nn22, 23), even though elsewhere he subordinates scientific claims to constructionist theory (e.g., 57, 61f, 101, 136, 181-90, 203 n11, 234 n27).

approach to homosexuality is rejected by postmodern theories and the various other forces of postmodern culture-formation or social construction: "Gay sexuality doesn't need to be legitimated by undergoing moral reform at the hands of liberalism! Homosexuals must remain 'queer,' and reject their mainstreaming into bourgeois society. Gay sex doesn't need to be reformed by straight sex! Straight sex needs to be revolutionized by gay sex!"[4]

In the phraseology of the famous Michel Foucault (1926-84), a defender of pedophilia[5] and a celebrant of sadomasochism in both theory and practice,[6] since there is not in homosexuals or in anybody else an *essence* that can be *liberated* from social conventions imposed counter to its nature, even the ideals of liberation and progress are rejected. Instead, the point is to be "transgressive" against the limits of your formation by such impositions; for in the on-going process of transgression and re-transgression

---

[4]Cf. Goss, 41, 113-41. Goss does, however, show some ambivalence on this matter, since he also demands an end to such "difference" by the mainstreaming of the principle that there ought to be no mainstream (cf Goss, 172-74). In this he reminds somewhat of Martin Heidegger's project to routinize, or bring into ordinariness, Being's hitherto unroutineness or extraordinariness, presumably in order to prepare a longing for the revelation of an unprecedented, radically discontinuous, and "sublime" extraordinary revelation (cf his *Introduction to Metaphysics* beginning).

[5]Cf. Macey, 255, 374-77; Michel Foucault, *The History of Sexuality, Volume 1: An Introduction* (Random House, 1980; trans., Robert Hurley), 31, 37; though contra Goss, 18, 200n69, 203n9, 218n30, but 68.

[6]Cf. Didier Eribon, *Michel Foucault* (Harvard University Press, 1991; trans., Betsy Wing), 315; David Macey, *The Lives of Michel Foucault* (Hutchinson, 1990), 355ff, 364-70; Goss, 157.

you find the essentially essenceless truth about yourself as a transgressor against whatever norms have shaped you.[7] For example, if proper self-respect is one of the ideals that have shaped you, then the point is for you to transgress that limit through the thrills of masochism in which you celebrate the affronting of your sense of self-worth. But a transgressor cannot remain a transgressor if he is liberated from all limiting impositions. Without such limitations he couldn't exist at all. So perhaps when all bourgeois standards have been transgressed and transgression seems to have become futureless, residual longings will induce post-post-modernists to re-impose Calvinism or other mediaeval values on bodiliness, in order that there will be new laws and rules, and transgression will become possible again.

According to radical postmodernism, essencelessness is true of conservative and liberal bourgeois Christians too, only they don't recognize it. But postmodernist revisions of Christian life are emerging (as from their unfair suppression by Bernard of Clairvaux and Francis of Assisi) and many Christian theologians are beginning to become Foucaultian in theory, though few have dared put it into practice yet. Guided by such self-understandings, postmodernism's routinely subversive authorities are undermining the traditional authority of liberalism's ideals, which are being replaced by a habit of anti-conformism. In postmodernism, then, there is an unspoken and perhaps unrecognized but nonetheless actual opposition to the normalization of homosexuality that old-fashioned liberalism advocates. Postmodernist theory and art (including

---

[7]Cf. Macey, 138, 256, 365, 368; Goss, 38-43, 147-56; Barry Cooper, *Michel Foucault: An Introduction to the Study of His Thought* (Edwin Mellen Press, 1981), 132. Foucault, *The Order of Things: An Archeology of the Human Sciences* (Random House, 1994), 328.

popular art and music) are socially constructing a culture of sexuality that affirms even sadomasochism, which political correctness commands us to call "SM" — i.e., the social production of I-thou thrills through violating and being violated, humiliating and being humiliated.[8] So far at least, classic liberals have done nothing to challenge the still-increasing authority of the Marquis de Sade, Michel Foucault, and other such transgression theorists at high-prestige universities (and seminaries). Perhaps postmodernists in secular society are not aware of the conservative-liberal tension within the churches. But if these theorists are aware of this tension, they seem content to see the ideal of gay monogamy used to dissolve conservatism's opposition to same-sex venery, without feeling themselves obliged to take monogamy and I-thou reverence seriously as ideals in the social construction of a post-homophobia future. Presumably it is necessary to bring residual conservative groups in Western society through a liberal phase before they can be opened up to postmodernism.

---

[8] I offer this definition as an objective or value-neutral description of sadomasochism, since these things are in fact what sadomasochists do for the sake of thrills. Fortunately, consent is still a condition for sadism, though there is no reason to suppose that Dionysos will continue indefinitely to submit to the principle of consent; for there might also be strong thrills in overwhelming volition in the other and/or in having one's volition overwhelmed by the other. In postmodernist theory, the self that upholds the principle of consent as its "center" is either an unselfknowing bourgeois-hypocritical mask which needs to be shaken, or perhaps is an ironic mask that invites subversion. Foucault backs away from the question of rape at least of a woman or an "unseductive" child by a man, but he can't or won't explain his hesitation to affirm such violence (Macey, 374-77).

Now, I don't know, but I doubt that old-fashioned liberal progressivism will some day succeed in bringing about an ethos of monogamy for gay sexuality similar to the ethos of marriage. For this to happen, liberalism would have to renew itself and regain its culture-forming power, and begin reversing the social impact of postmodernism in pop culture and high theory at prestige universities, and the transgressive sexual politics of Queer Nation and similar movements. At present, all these forces are now socially constructing sexuality—especially homosexuality—in directions very much opposed to the ideals of liberalism, which has always exhorted individuals to self-restraint and otherwise moral behavior. Yes, "marginal" religious movements have sometimes produced great transformations at the centers of social power, but this result is hardly to be assumed as a matter of course. The marginal ends up "transforming history" only when something developing at the margins of power (for example, Christian monotheism, or the work ethic that developed in Calvinist backwaters) is found to be necessary at the centre of power (for example, the Roman Empire, or technological Europe). And since the leading opinion-forming institutions have been turning away from individualism and reason, it doesn't look like they are groping around for an articulation of old-fashioned liberal ethical monotheism. So I doubt liberal Christians should assume as a matter of course that the goodness of their intentions are some kind of guarantee that their intentions will prevail—especially when they are still trying to see in Foucaultian thought some kind of ally in their struggle against conservative Christianity.[9] Christian liberals like Mel White put quote-marks around "liberal" as if it is at

---

[9]Cf. J. Mills, "Morally Dionysian Religious Authority vs. *The Rules.*" 33:1 *Crux* (Mar. 1997; 22-30).

best a problematic term.[10] White even interprets the proponents of postmodernist sexuality as cloaked supporters of the idea that social forces probably maybe ought to construct a humane monogamous ethos for homosexual individuals.[11] The prospects for a renewal of liberal Christian morality are not bright—especially when it comes to homosexuality.

Some conservatives might suppose that I am laughing here over liberal Christianity's dissolution by postmodernist theory. But I ask them to think what the dissolution of liberalism might mean in law and government. The proponents of postmodernism are hardly concentrating their efforts on the subversion of liberalism at Protestant and Catholic seminaries. Moreover, many ideals (for example, the sanctity of the individual's conscience) are shared by liberal and conservative Christians. Conservative Christians ought not to view the dissolution of such ideals—for example, at law schools—so complacently. To this extent, I am actually very sorry there is so little likelihood that liberal Christians will awaken to the reality that their ideals are engaged in a cultural war with postmodernism—and that they must think how to win this war. On the other hand, the new "conservative" ideals of marriage and family remain appealing as respectful of individuals regardless of their "orientation."

---

[10]Mel White, 76.

[11]Mel White, 68f. Contrast Goss, passim, especially 57ff, 62, 136, 177ff, 190, 205n31, 234n27. Of course, conservatives could easily deflect postmodernist critique by ironically adopting the social constructionist theory: "If everything human is social construction, what's amiss if we socially construct traditional marriages or produce other sorts of conservatism?"

Chapter 16

Enduring This Unnoticed "Cultural War"

Actually, it surprises me that this cultural war between liberalism and postmodernism over the future of "sexuality" isn't more noticed and analyzed. If Judeo-Christian and secularist liberals wished to become the authoritative interpreters of "sexuality," they would have to start noticing and analyzing their primary challengers, who are not religio-moral conservatives but postmodernists. Conservative opposition to homosexuality (an opposition now becoming culturally marginal) is actually no obstacle at all to a gathering of gay men and lesbians around a clarion call to monogamous idealism and the remnants of ethical monotheism. Admittedly, such a clarion call might have little if any culture-forming power. My point is that conservatives are not preventing liberals from sounding forth such a call. Moreover, since liberals are doing nothing to rally gay and lesbian sexuality around the banner of liberal ethical monotheism, it's unreasonable for liberals to insist that we conservatives "dialogue" with them as though they were trying to form an ethos of old-fashioned liberal morality for gays and lesbians. In fact, it would be quite reasonable for us conservatives to request that liberals decide amongst themselves where they stand on things modern and things postmodern, so we conservatives could have some notion

of whom we are to be "in dialogue" with. Are we conservatives being called to an old-fashioned moral liberal position on homosexual relationships—like Helmut Theilicke's
view—as a mere prelude to a Foucaultian, postmodernist
view?

Liberal progressivists are actually at cross-purposes
with postmodernists over the issue of "orientation
change." Liberals like Mel White argue from Enlightenment science that "sexual orientation" is unchangeable on
the one hand because of sexuality's genetics and on the
other hand because of the irreversibility of sexuo-personal
development induced by various environmental factors
during childhood. For liberals, since science shows orientation is unchangeable, homosexuals ought to express it in
"responsible" gay relationships beginning in early teenage
years.[1] Of course, early sexual exploration is congruent

---

[1]White, 33-35, 69, 72, 104, 134. Of course, even in view of secular evidence, one may doubt that early experimentation in sexual relationships for "homosexual" teenagers could be helpful
in their emotional and psychological development, even when
older males do not initiate such experimentation (as also older
males involve themselves in much "heterosexual" experimentation). According to research done on teenage heterosexuality,
schoolwork and graduation correlate with *postponing* relationships of venery: William H. Masters, et al, *Heterosexuality*, 445,
449. Of course, it is possible that although postponing venery
helps rather than harms psychological development and matu-
ration in adolescent boys and girls in *heterosexual* relationships,
the reverse might be true for teenage boys in relationships
among themselves. But before recommending, as does White,
that churches and schools advise adolescent boys to begin such
relationships, liberals really ought to investigate whether such
relationships really will foster rather than undermine matura-
tion, self-discipline in schoolwork, and participation in the full
breadth of social life. The developmentally disorienting impact
Continued . . .

with postmodernism, which affirms various "constructionist" notions. These notions teach that sexual identity is
something fluid and changeable, which dons and doffs
varying historical "masks" or "personae." Orientation
change is opposed by postmodernists not on grounds that
Enlightenment science shows it to be impossible but on
grounds that there is no point in trying to become
"straight" to begin with. In this way, postmodernism actually ends up providing encouragement for "homosexuals" who wish to change their "orientation" — for purposes that may be condemned by postmodern theorists,
but that "homosexual" men themselves may find very
appealing nevertheless (marriage, love, family). For example, Robert Goss, formerly a Jesuit but now a disciple
of Michel Foucault, concurs exactly with conservative
Christian proponents of orientation change when he says,
"It is difficult."[2]

In any case, in the current situation of ethos-lessness in
the gay and lesbian "community," it should be no wonder
that lots — in any case an undiscoverable number — of men
with strong venereal desires toward men find marriage
and family more appealing than any alternative, even
when they are not believers in the biblical God. And if they
are believers in the biblical God, they will find marriage
and family all the more meaningful as life purposes. With
such purposes and belonging in view, when such men decide for marriage and family, there's no need to explain
this decision as the expression of "internalized homopho-

---

that failing to postpone sexual relations has on heterosexual
teenagers may be even *worse* in the context of homosexual relations among teenage boys, for easily discoverable causes: cf
Randy Shilts, *And the Band Played On: Politics, People and the
AIDS Epidemic* (St Martin's Press, 1987), 20, 28, 46, 89.
[2]Goss, 7f; cf 234, but 12.

bia." Christian gay liberationism is today an incoherent, confused, and confusing mix of various classical liberal ideals and postmodernist theories and impulses. As for any need for "dialogue" between conservative Christians and liberationist Christians, shouldn't liberationist Christians first decide among themselves whether they wish to be classical liberals or postmodernists? That way, conservatives could know whether their dialogue partners are trying to return to ethical monotheism or are following Foucault and others into the world night preceding the dawn of a postmodern era. I daresay, however, that my complaint that today's Christian pro-gay message is incoherent is likely to be suppressed by typical postmodernist notions: "Disorder and fluctuations are the source and possibility of creativity, not of decay and confusion. Indeterminacy, disturbance, oscillation, and imbalance do not *close* our horizons but *open* them. If conservative Christians find themselves 'confused' by a pro-gay message that refuses logocentrism, this indicates a failure not in Christian gay liberationism but in Christian conservatives, since they cannot live in the richness of disequilibrium."

I guess I end this interlude as an "absent signifier" for "polyvalent hegemony" or something, but I call any genuinely "mobile readers" to press on with me into a consideration of Jean-Jacques Rousseau. It seems to me it is with Rousseau (1712-78) that Western culture began its thoughtless drift into the opinion that marriage is an "expression of heterosexuality" and that "homosexuals" must be excluded from marriage.

Chapter 17

Rousseau's Romanticism of the Sexes, and its Lasting Cultural Influence

B ut if the new understanding of marriage as an "expression" of "sexuality" does not derive from the Bible, where does it come from? It does not appear in Graeco-Roman antiquity. The Greeks and Romans spoke of sexual desires and actions as "aphroditic" or "venereal" after the goddess named Aphrodite among the Greeks and Venus among the Romans. I have tried to follow such usage in this booklet as much as possible. "Venery" and "venereal" may also involve misunderstandings, but at least their strangeness to our ears and eyes might encourage us to think more carefully what we do mean and what the truth actually is about these realities. In contrast to present-day theorists, the ancients did not see the desire for "venery" or "aphrodisia" in everything human beings do and say and think: Aphrodite/Venus was only one of their many deities, and she wasn't the highest deity. Certainly the Greeks and Romans did not define themselves as having an aphroditic "identity" or a venereal "orientation."

The question of what to do about the desire for "venery" of various sorts was something about which pre-Christian antiquity never could agree, especially as eastern mystery religions began to spread through the Roman empire. In that culture there were staunch supporters of extreme asceticism, staunch supporters of extreme licentiousness, staunch supporters of various middle courses, as well as staunch supporters of extreme asceticism who were unable to restrain themselves from extreme licentiousness.[1] It is enough for me here to emphasize that the ancients certainly did not consider the "aphroditic things" or "venery" to be the foundation of marriage or the basis of a human being's "identity." In fact, not Aphrodite/Venus but Hera/Juno was the goddess of marriage and family. It is also worth noting that Christianity seems to have brought a very important change to Graeco-Roman culture in the doctrine of women's moral and spiritual equality with men; "in Christ there is neither male nor female" (Gal 3:28) elevates women to the point where a man need not be ashamed to consider his wife his friend.

But if today's understanding of men and women as "sexual beings" with "sexual identities" and "sexual orientations" derives neither from the Bible nor from Graeco-Roman antiquity, where does this notion come from? I argue that it derives from Jean-Jacques Rousseau, the enormously influential Swiss-born French philosopher of the late Enlightenment era who invented the idea of marriage as a romanticism *of sexuality,* though even he does not use the term "sexuality." Rousseau was one of those few great minds that are not mere analyzers of things but are

---

[1]Cf., e.g., Reay Tannahill, *Sex in History* (Stein and Day, 1982), 84-135.

founders of radically new ways of understanding human beings and thus become powerful social constructors and shapers of culture.[2]

Prior to Rousseau, there were love stories, love songs, romances about adultery and other adventures, as well as ethical and religious celebrations of marriage. But no one had thought to form monogamous friendship and partnership from the bio-mechanics of the *sex drives* until Rousseau wrote *Julie, the New Heloise* (1761), the first novel of sexual romanticism, and *Emile* (1762), his novelistic anti-bourgeois sex education manual. As Paul Johnson puts it, "all our modern ideas of education are af-

---

[2]I contend that there are many defects in Allan Bloom's grandly sweeping statement of the meaning of our time in the context of "Jerusalem and Athens" (cf my note in 26:1 *Crux* [Mar., 1990], 37-42). Even his way of reading Rousseau seems flawed. But I think Bloom doesn't overstate Rousseau's impact: *The Closing of the American Mind* (Simon & Schuster, 1987), 167-70, 181-85, 298-300, 305; and *Love and Friendship* (Simon & Schuster, 1993), 39-156. Those influenced by Bloom's assessment of Rousseau include: Kant, *Kant on History* (Bobbs-Merrill, 1963; ed., Lewis White Beck), 56-63; Hegel, *Philosophy of Right* ¶¶ 29, 153 (addition), 258; Marx, *The Marx-Engels Reader*, second edition (W.W. Norton, 1978; ed., Robert Tucker), 46; Nietzsche, *Human, All Too Human* ¶¶ 463, 617; *Mixed Opinions and Maxims* ¶ 408; *Schopenhauer as Educator* ¶ 4; *Dawn of Morning* pref 3, ¶427; *Twilight of the Idols* x 48; *Will to Power* ¶¶ 62, 94, 1021; Karl Löwith, *From Hegel to Nietzsche: The Revolution in Nineteenth-Century Thought* (Columbia University Press, 1964; trans., David E. Green), 34, 164, 177f, 246, 235-43, 260; Karl Barth, *Protestant Thought: From Rousseau to Ritschl* (Ayer Company, 1959; trans., Brian Cozens), 58ff, 99-101 (on Goethe's dependence upon Rousseau), 151.

fected to some degree by Rousseau's doctrine, especially by his treatise *Emile.*" [3]

Why did Rousseau turn to human sexuality this way? He was not given to monogamy himself, though he definitely had a wide-open "heterosexual lifestyle." On a largely secularistic but slightly Deistic basis, Rousseau tried to defeat the emerging "bourgeois" individualism that we now associate with "Enlightenment rationality" and "capitalism." He was alarmed that in bourgeois society all relationships between human beings, especially marriages, were becoming determined by contracts based in the calculation of selfish interests.

In such calculation, I ask myself about every proposed interaction with an other "What's in it for me?" I ask this question within the assumption that my interests and thy interests never agree naturally but only by economic or prestige calculation. For example, I, a wood-cutter, have no natural need to give lumber to thee; and thou, a house-builder, hast no natural need to build me a house. But since thou needest lumber and since I need a house, we can work out a deal, so that I supply thee with lumber for the houses thou buildest and thou suppliest me with a house. However, if I don't need a house built by thee, I have no motive to be in community with thee. In this way, any I-thou is nothing more than "I scratch thy back and thou scratchest mine." For efficiency's sake, of course, such mutually beneficial contracting is streamlined by the convention of money. Family, friendship, citizenship, and every other sort of human interaction gets interpreted in light of such dealing; all others become for me instruments to be used for increasing my own power, prestige, pleasure, comfort, wealth, and the like. So, in Rousseau's view, any "common good" between people is an artificial con-

---

[3]Paul Johnson, *Intellectuals* (Weidenfeld & Nicolson, 1988), 3.

struct, not based in a natural or organic unity. The only exception is for sexual interactions, when formed and channelled by the cultural and educational system he envisioned. Human sexuality was to be the one exception to ordinary selfishness, the one way for the self to stand against the modern world's bourgeois-capitalistic structures.

Rousseau was one of the first to see that the individualism of the emerging technological society was dissolving the organic interconnectedness of parish life, the sacred family bonds of husband and wife, parents and children, and the surroundings of extended family and neighbors time out of mind. Now, he might have found an exit here by looking to the God of Abraham, Isaac, and Jacob for a covenantal existence for people who must be "strangers in a strange land" — as indeed everybody becomes in technological society. Believers in the God of the Scriptures can turn to the intentionality of faith, of covenant, and upbuilding in the grace of the Holy Spirit. But although raised a Calvinist, Rousseau was a Deist: the famous Modernist (liberal) Catholic "Faith Statement of the Savoyard Vicar" forms part of *Emile*.[4] Therefore, Rousseau did not turn to the Bible for our Divine gathering into a common life. Instead he tried to forge a new way of belonging for us out of our sexualness. His plan was, as we'd say today, to "socially construct" our sexualness into the lifeblood of "family values."

It seems Rousseau believed everybody is spontaneously, naturally heterosexual in orientation, and that human sexualness goes in other directions only when corrupted by bourgeois civilization.[5] Certainly he did not

---

[4]*Emile* (Basic Books, 1979; trans., Allan Bloom), 266-313.
[5]*Emile*, 214, 317. Cf. also *The First and Second Discourses* (Harper and Row, 1985; trans. Victor Gourevitch), 142, 164-66; *Confes-
Continued . . .

worry that homosexual desires will emerge in the boy (Emile) he educates from childhood to adulthood, even though he arranges for Emile to pass almost his entire adolescence without seeing a woman. Rousseau's doctrine thus provides the basis for subsequent attempts by modern psychiatric technique to "restore" in "homosexuals" the "heterosexual orientation" that can be assumed to be naturally, spontaneously operative in all human organisms from their conception.[6] For Rousseau, human nature is not fallen; "degeneracies" can exist in human beings only by the deforming influences of human society. In contrast, traditional Christian doctrine merely forbade venery between men on grounds that venery's only permissible context is marriage. No traditional authority commanded the obliteration of "homosexual" lust and the extorting of "heterosexual" lust from oneself—as though such lust ought to exist in a man by nature according to God's original design.

Rousseau's doctrine that the anti-individualist partnership of woman and man in marriage must be an expression of sexuality would also seem to be the remote source for the opinion that homosexuals are more narcissistic than heterosexuals or even that homosexualness is a kind of male narcissism. Ample refutation for this opinion, however, is provided by Rousseau's own (hetero-

---

sions (Wordsworth Editions, 1996), 64. This view was upheld by Marx and his followers.
[6]Davies and Rentzel's Rousseauan assertion that a homosexual orientation "is, at its root, a symptom of unmet emotional needs" (68; cf 85) conflicts with their Christian realism about the enduring impact of the fall and with their belief that heterosexual lust does not often emerge in the course of therapy and prayer for change, no matter how well former homosexuals learn to find fulfilment for their emotional needs (94-9).

sexual) narcissism in thought and deed,[7] to say nothing of heterosexual narcissism, for example, in pop music stars — which is a heterosexualness free to express itself sponanteously. A "homosexual lifestyle" is indeed likely to seem meaningless and narcissistic in comparison with marriage and family, but a "heterosexual lifestyle" — consider the connotations of the word "playboy" — is also likely to appear meaningless and narcissistic in comparison with marriage and family. Today we cannot repeat too often that marriage is not an "expression of heterosexuality." It is a covenantal relationship.

Now, since in Rousseau's eyes the most degraded human condition is individualism (economic self-aggrandizement, careerist egotism), all effort is made to prevent Emile from sexual self-release or "ipsation" (the term in traditional moral theology for solitary, as contrasted with mutual, masturbation). According to Rousseau, only our sex drives can bring us out of individualism and into the genuine community of husband and wife. If you ipsate during your sexuo-personal development during adolescence, you will emerge as an adult with no motive for entering such community. You will be capable of only a contractual marriage of interests between two separate, individualistic selves.

Since Emile's marriage to Sophie (a young woman also subjected in the novel to Rousseau's educational theories) is to be an expression of his (hetero) sexuality in a genuinely communal relationship, Rousseau argues it would be much better for Emile to hire a prostitute for the release of his sexual tension than to ipsate, since prostitution at least involves interaction between self and other, whereas

---

[7]Johnson, 1-27.

ipsation does not.[8] Thus, with Rousseau's *Emile* began the hysterical drive in educators, parenthood experts and medical practitioners in the nineteenth century[9] to prevent youngsters from ipsation. This hysteria was driven basically by the belief that sexual self-release causes narcissism and organic degeneracy, but to this belief were added traditional religio-moral rules. While Victorian anti-ipsation hysteria has now subsided, Rousseau's influence is still seen today when conservative authorities teach less that refraining from ispation is a duty imposed upon young and old alike by moral law (as, for example, Aquinas taught), than that ipsation endangers adolescents' emotional and psychological development by turning them in on themselves and away from the normal social actions in which they must participate in order to mature. In this way a doctrine of duty has been exchanged for a doctrine turning on practical questions (whether self-release has certain developmental results or not).[10]

---

[8]*Emile*, 333f; cf 265-67; also Rousseau's *Confessions* iii (beginning).

[9]Cf. Foucault, 28-30, 42.

[10]Rousseau's strictures against ipsation on grounds that it is motivated by and reinforces narcissism or an "inordinate self-love" can still be seen in, for example, Johann Christoph Arnold, *A Plea for Purity: Sex, Marriage & God* (Plough, 1996), 108-110; Leanne Payne, *The Broken Image: Restoring Personal Wholeness Through Healing Prayer* (Crossway Books, 1981), 91f; Karol Wojtyla, *The Splendor of Truth* ¶47 ("auto-eroticism"); Vittorio Messori, ed., *The Ratzinger Report: An Exclusive Interview on the State of the Church* (Ignatius Press, 1985; trans., Salvator Attanasio, Graham Harrison), 87.

Yet even if I have convinced some conservatives that we have erred greatly in accepting Rousseau's understanding of *marriage* as an expression of sexuality, many readers may suppose that Rousseau's arguments against *ipsation* remain sound, *Continued . . .*

even though these readers do not concur in the judgment of Rousseau and St. Augustine that prostitution (i.e., "heterosexual" prostution) may be condoned instead as the necessary remedy for male lust, which I venture to say is especially unsuitable for teenage males. But to me it seems fortunate that conservative Christian authorities have begun to teach that ispation is right for the pragmatic remedying of lust; cf, e.g., Lewis B. Smedes, *Sex For Christians* (Eerdmans, 1976), 162, 246; Stanley Grenz, *Sexual Ethics: A Biblical Perspective* (Word Publishing, 1990), 190f. By teaching that ipsation is a remedy for lust rather than an indulgence in it, such newer conservative authorities differ from traditional authorities like Aquinas, who treats ipsation as done only by those that give themselves over to the incontinent seeking of pleasure (*Summa Theologica* 2-2 q154 a11).

But as valid as necessary self-release for adolscents might seem in the opinion of some conservatives, some parents and educators might fear that giving teenage boys permission even for *necessary* ipsation might result in harmful psychological developments: "These youngsters might exceed the bounds of necessity and develop a mindset of pleasure-seeking. Perhaps parents who fail to forbid even seemingly necessary ipsation will foster in their young sons a more or less complete inability to withstand any venereal temptation, who therefore will give themselves over to pre-marital sex; hence, although the forbidding of ipsation is not likely to be entirely successful, only if parents and other authorities prohibit even the least practice that involves venereal pleasure will youngsters be able to build up the internal barriers of shame and guilt from which (some might suppose) self-control is constructed." Yet these are practical questions, whose answers can be found by investigation. For example, when ipsation is compulsive and draws a teenager away from social activities at school and church, his difficulty is not insufficient guilt and shame but excessive amounts (Smedes, 163f; David Crawford, *Easing the Ache: Gay Men Recovering From Compulsive Behaviors* [Dutton, 1990], 34-40). Obsessive ipsation *Continued . . .*

in adolescents or adults is best helped by the techniques of cognitive and behavioral therapy, not exhortations about "becoming normal."

For the same reasons, having to try always to be refraining from self-release (until his marriage, which he must suppose is yet years and years away and in any case probably should not be looked upon as a relationship entered into for the sake of such release), far from preventing "inordinate self-love," only makes a teenager more self-involved and narcissistic. For him, self-release is not an exercise in self-love or "auto-eroticism" but a way of enabling himself to attend to his homework or other tasks with greater focus and attention. It also helps him to refrain from staring impolitely at the sexiest girls (or guys) in his classes. In sum, learning to "take responsibility for his own sexual needs" neither deflects his social development into an embarrassing introversion nor drives him into pre-marital sex, but enables him to "get on with his life." Learning to "take care of one's own sexual needs" during adolescence would also seem to be necessary if a man is to be sensitive to his wife's inclinations and disinclinations, rather than selfishly foisting his drives upon her as though she is his remedy for lust.

Though I cannot concur in her approach to the Bible, and though she has no notion of males' resistance to any routine use of condoms, cf on these questions, Meg Hickling, *Speaking of Sex: Are You Ready to Answer the Questions Your Kids Will Ask?* (Northstone, 1996). As Thomas E. Schmidt notes, "it does not require a degree in behavioral research to guess" why sexually transmitted diseases are spreading; it is not that sex-ed programs have been insufficiently funded, but that "Men do not like to wear condoms" (*Straight and Narrow? Compassion and Clarity in the Homosexuality Debate* [InterVarsity, 1995], 125. Cf. also Masters et al, 443-46, 451-53; Barbara Dafoe Whitehead, "The Failure of Sex Education" in 274:4 *The Atlantic Monthly*, 55-80.

There is also a far graver consideration here. In today's wide-open society with young teenagers so often left in unsupervised *Continued . . .*

In this way Rousseau attempted to initiate a culture-forming project to take what he supposed is our natural heterosexualness from earliest childhood and to shape it into the sexual expression called marriage. There is no place for laughter about venery (or, I think, about anything else!) in *Emile* or in *Julie*—probably because Rousseau believed it is only through pretensiousness about human sexualness that there can be genuine human interconnectedness. Laughing at the laughable realities in human sexualness would dissolve his whole project, and

---

environments, it seems important, even urgent, to teach both male and female teenagers that they must gain self-knowledge in their "sexuality" and "take responsibility for their own sexual needs" also in order to make them less vulnerable to predatory adults who understand their desires better than they do. Parents averse to this advice would do well to take as a warning this remark by the Rev. Robert Williams: "it is a vocation, an important responsibility—and, at some level, an honor" to seduce young people suspected of having the capacity to find homosexual venery thrilling, in order to prove to these young people that they must express and celebrate their gay sexual identity, and that there's no point in marriage and family for them (*Just as I Am*, 175).

Conservatives who wish still to maintain that ipsation even for a good purpose (e.g., attending to math homework) is always an intrinsically and gravely disordered action should ask themselves really whether they would have religious and moral authorities teach this to a man who is turning to self-release for the sake of ceasing to hire prostitutes, staying away from gay bars, or avoiding foisting his sexualness upon people in his pastoral care. Neither adult nor teenager is likely to be strengthened in "taking responsibility for his own sexual needs" by interpreting for him his turning to self-release as perhaps less than entirely culpable because of an embarrassing "affective immaturity" in him or because of the control of his personality by other "psychological or social factors."

we'd be left (as Rousseau supposes) with only calculating bourgeois individualism in sexuality, as in everything else. For C.S. Lewis, on the other hand—not to mention Shakespeare—any humanly appropriate treatment of venery, even in the highest contexts in which it can appear, must include a sense of its ridiculous aspects.[11]

I must say Rousseau's was a strange plan, since of course what was still at that time called "lust" is something we can readily use in our calculations how to exploit others for our own economic, pleasure, and prestige interests. Sexualness would seem to be far more likely to deflect love *toward* narcissism than to make love possible to begin with. Certainly, capitalism has been able to market the objects of lust as never before. How could our "sex drives" really be the foundation of "family values" and a genuinely human interpersonal belonging! Yet Rousseau actually argued that the formation of the human sex drive through imagination and culture[12] could create relationships of genuine belonging between husband and wife, and that these relationships would also provide a stable and warm environment for the raising of children. Rousseau reasoned that he did not have to try to obey his own doctrine since his sexuality was too corrupted by bourgeois society (not by the Fall and original sin) for him to find monogamy for the sake of child-raising a satisfying way of life.[13] But he tried to redeem others' corrupted sexuality into the basis of a humanly meaningful monogamy despite the modern system of calculation. According

---

[11]Cf. *The Four Loves*, 22, 37, 90-94, 103; *The Screwtape Letters* #11. The noble love between Romeo and Juliet does not require the repression of such venereal realities as are emphasized by Mercutio and Nurse.

[12]*Emile* 328f, 357ff, 488f.

[13]Cf. Paul Johnson, 21-23.

to Rousseau, a genuine "I and Thou against the world" can have no basis but "sexualness between me and thee."

The realist in me scoffs at this educational project, and I'm actually astonished that anyone could ever have thought it could work. But the *idealist* in me also scoffs at this project: what poverty of soul is required in order to conclude there is no belonging but what derives from sexualness?[14] Yet Rousseau's romanticism of monogamous heterosexualness caught the fancy of many and quickly pervaded Western culture. Romanticism based in the shaping of our spontaneous sexualness seemed to promise both an escape from individualism and liberation from the hassle of externally imposed rules and insincere con-

---

[14]Beside Rousseau's sexual romanticism there is also his equally epochal foundations of the modern politics of radical egalitarianism based in the natural appeal of compassion served by unlimited state power (*Of the Social Contract* in conjunction with *Discourse on the Origin and the Foundations of Inequality Among Men*). In addition, right-wing anti-"decadence" demos-based politics owes a lot to Rousseau (*Of the Social Contract* in conjunction with *Discourse on the Sciences and the Arts* and *Letter on the Theatre*). He says in the preface to his Discourse on inequality: "What experiments would be needed in order to come to know natural man; and by what means can these experiments be performed within society? ... I believe that I have meditated upon the subject sufficiently to dare answer in advance that the greatest philosophers will not be too good to direct these experiments, nor the most powerful sovereigns to perform them." Experimenting for such idealism becomes so irresistable for opinion leaders and revolutionaries that Nietzsche remarks (in his own blood-curdling way) on the future of communist and national socialisms that such idealism can be refuted only by a massive "practical instruction" through "a few great experiments" that result in "a tremendous expenditure of human lives" (*Will to Power* ¶125).

ventionalities. No longer would we have to accept rules and institutions of any sort as showing us "who we are." For his romantic notion of the love between the sexes and for his ethical theories in general, Rousseau was proclaimed "the Newton of the moral realm" by no less a thinker than Immanuel Kant.[15]

Of course, as anybody can see by looking around himself—and perhaps within himself —Rousseau's reform project failed, and today the romanticism of sexuality has only disappointed devotees. It is no longer a powerful idealism, except in its deconstructed postmodernist forms. But because Western societies haven't found an idealism to replace the Rousseauan romanticism which no one any longer really believes in, our ideas about marriage remain the decayed remnants of Rousseau's vision for sexual belonging. So even today we continue to socially construct ourselves in accord with Rousseau's basic idea when we use the word "heterosexual" or "homosexual" or perhaps "bisexual" and interpret ourselves as having a "sexual identity." It is as though we still suppose that Tolstoy's famous question "What should we do and how should we live?" is somehow best answered "Thou shalt express thy sexuality!" Even though no one believes a "heterosexual" man is *actually* attached to his wife because of his sexualness, we still consider marriage an "expression of heterosexuality"—at least to the extent that "homosexual" men must be excluded from it, which is something no society before our own has ever asserted.

But Tolstoy's question is not decided for us by our venereal inclinations.[16] It is in our hearts that we human beings must think and decide how to live. The notion of

---

[15]*Kant's Political Writings* (Cambridge University Press, 1977; ed., Hans Reiss; trans., H.B. Nisbet), 4.
[16]Contra Mel White, 261.

"sexual identity," however, is used by gay liberationism to insist that "a homosexual" has not only the right but almost the duty to (choose to) express these desires, since they are "who he is." This duty holds even for husbands and fathers. No one with any concern about what's good and right believes that a "heterosexual" man should abandon his children and his decreasingly erotically interesting wife, in order to enjoy "meaningful" sexual experiences with another woman or women. It goes without saying among liberationists, however, that a man who is married and has children yet who comes to realize that he "is" a homosexual (would find venery with men thrilling) ought to leave his marriage and seek meaningful homosexual relationships – as long as he at least recognizes that the expression of his true sexual being will be difficult for his wife and children.[17] This is part of the price we are still paying for accepting Rousseau's influence.[18] If we

---

[17]Mel White sustains this doctrine even when one's wife is one's "best and closest friend" and does not wish to end the marriage (cf 73, 75, 86f, 98, 117f, 149f, 162f, 180, 185, 190, 212f). There are many thoroughly "heterosexual" married men that do not have as loving, meaningful, and even sexual (87, 177) a marriage as did White.

[18]Presumably Rousseau's notion that a man is to be basically bound to his wife through his sexualness is also the remote source for the belief that a man's sexualness, when it veers away from his wife, validates abandoning her and the children: it is dishonest and insincere to remain with one's wife when one no longer finds her sexually satisfying. For Rousseau, human beings are basically good, and human beings are basically sexual; so sexuality is basically good. So, today, guided by feminism, our culture tells us to define rape as "a crime of violence, not sexuality." Yet we still speak of "sex crimes." And it is the sexualness of the violence involved in rape and other sexual assaults that makes such crimes so humanly damaging, even *Continued* . . .

removed Rousseau's notions of sexual identity from our culture, how would we understand venery or the things of Aphrodite? I suggest what is left is a set of various desires that everybody has to learn how to live with. And the Gospel can tell us how, if we discover how to free ourselves from our residual Rousseauanism.

---

when bodily tissues aren't harmed. Thus, human sexualness seems to be itself warpable by evil, rather than being a mere tool of evil and remaining something necessarily non-violent in itself. Moreover, it is precisely in the violation and being violated that sadomasochism is found so sexually thrilling. Only in late modernity could sadomasochists demand bourgeois respectability and the status of a "community" — and have bourgeois authorities cave in to this demand for societal and moral respectability!

Chapter 18

In Defense of "Orientation Change" Ministries and Therapies

Now, some Christian conservatives will say I'm inventing a problem here since they believe that not only "homosexual behavior" but also "homosexual orientation" is usually or even perhaps always changeable by some combination of moral effort, psychotherapy, prayer, and the healing power of the Holy Spirit. The idea is that with persistence along these lines, homosexual men will find that they can be restored to the "normal" sexuality (heterosexuality—desire for venery with all attractive women), which is the only permissible doorway to marriage and family. Other conservatives, however, including me, believe that a man's venereal desires very often or even usually prove unchangeable in their primary "orientation." I agree that "homosexuality" was not in God's original design for the human race, but I also maintain that "heterosexuality" was not in God's original design either.

So I'd argue that a "homosexual orientation" and a (fallen) "heterosexual orientation" are morally and religiously equivalent.[1] A "homosexually oriented" man is not more fallen than a "heterosexually oriented" man. This means both heterosexual lust and homosexual lust are "normal" in *fallen* male human beings, though neither avenue of lust should be affirmed since neither is what God intended. In my opinion, every Christian male must find his own repeatedly revised pathway that involves both repentance for lusting, and shrugging off the effects of the Fall on his desires: he must find a way to pass between the Scylla of attempting to "mortify" his venereal desire and the Charybdis of "celebrating" it. In this task, the man whose venereal desires are entirely or exclusively focused on women faces much the same challenges as the man whose venereal desires are focused entirely or exclusively on men. Whether our venereal desires are focused

---

[1]This equivalence, however, should not become a new ranking system, in which men whose venereal drives are fixated on other forbidden things (I won't specify them, since I'd only leave some out) are rated as worse human beings than men venereally oriented toward female or male adults. If such men restrain their sexual desires, they deserve respect, not contempt. The prevailing use of the term "normal" is always very misleading in these contexts. On the one hand, it permits the user to introduce value judgments: "normal" feelings and behavior presumably call for no shame, but "abnormal" feelings and behavior probably do call for some shame. But "normal" also involves some kind of claim to scientific objectivity that transcends particular religio-moral horizons. So the weight and authority of empirical science is — intentionally or not — brought down upon men who are deemed "abnormal" in one way or another — even when they are making valiant efforts to do what is good and right. Let us remember that God judges by deeds and perceives the intention of the heart. He does not evaluate human beings by deciding how "normal" or "abnormal" we are!

more on men or more on women, we may wish that the Holy Spirit would restore these desires to the natural, spontaneous monogamy of the Garden of Eden. But it seems to me the path of salvation usually involves finding out how to live with the effects of the Fall on our venereal desires.

Unfortunately, the "normal fallenness" both of venereal desire for all attractive women *and* of venereal desire for all attractive men is not accepted by many conservative Christians. No teenage boy has cause to lie awake at night in fear he will be beaten at school or even exiled from his family if someone discovers he dreams of being a Porsche-driving servant of Mammon. This is not so, however, for the teenage boy who discovers "homosexual" urges in himself. If a teenage boy mentions being troubled by the power of heterosexual urges in him, even conservative counsellors and parents will reassure him that these desires are "normal." But few will reassure a teenage boy who mentions desires toward other males that he is nonetheless a "normal" guy. Therefore, many adult and adolescent males with strong venereal desires toward males believe the presence of such desire proves not only that they are somehow uniquely fallen and rejected by God, but also that they are rightly excluded from hearth and home, marriage and family, the primary arrangements in which men find purpose and belonging as well as social acceptance and some kind of order for their lives.

It is usually only by loving one woman and becoming the father of her children that men are able to elevate themselves out of the disarray that is maleness left to itself.[2] We shouldn't wonder if closing marriage against

---

[2] Cf. Davies and Rentzel, 182; George Gilder, *Sexual Suicide* (Quadrangle, 1972), passim; *Wealth and Poverty* (Basic Books, 1981), 87-95.

"homosexually oriented" men leaves them in a state of social and personal paralysis when they find the orientation of their venereal desires unchanged. And it should be no surprise that suicidal depression and self-hatred can be induced in men and adolescents when they come to believe that the orientation of their drives for venery deprives them of the right to marry and raise a family. The persistence — despite all prayer and moral effort — of the orientation of his drives for venery toward men might even prompt him to conclude that he is excluded from God's grace.[3] Admittedly, many men decide to go ahead and get married anyway, telling no one of their "sexual identity." What motivates them is not "internalized homophobia" but the entirely reasonable wish to enjoy the benefits of marriage and family despite the prohibition extended to such men by the opinion prevailing in our culture. Their on-going strength and courage is remarkable, but it is unfortunate that our culture imposes upon them the entirely false belief that the truth about their "identity" implies that they are living fraudulent lives. They may hesitate even to pray to God for strength and grace to persevere since Christian liberalism and Christian conservatism conspire together to tell them that God considers it wrong of them to have married to begin with. So, unless they have unusual independence of mind, they are likely to conclude that God is hardly likely to support them in their life paths.

But the persistence of strong desires for venery with men is no more an indication of abandonment by God than is the "persistence" of heterosexuality. What we call

---

[3]It seems it was this belief, not the duty of refraining from homosexual behavior, that so tormented Mel White (14, 73, 98, 105, 133, 199), especially since he easily accepts that two gay men cannot long find venery between them exciting (261).

"heterosexuality" as it is experienced after the Fall is not what God intended for us either. Let's consider the situation of the "heterosexual" male caught up in pornography on the Internet, in sex addiction with prostitutes, or in a meaningless and even sickening yet seemingly irresistible affair with a co-worker or his best friend's wife. Such a man doesn't expect Divine intervention and a miracle to redirect his venereal desire toward his own wife. He knows his own effort is required, and hence he prays for another kind of Divine grace. Similarly, we should recognize that God doesn't—at least not as a matter of course—miraculously intervene to re-direct toward women the venereal desires of men today called "homosexual."

The only attempt to describe unfallen, Edenic venereal desire that I know of is C.S. Lewis' account of monogamy among the *hrossa* in the twelfth chapter of *Out of the Silent Planet* (1938). This love is very unpassionate in one way, but meditative and poetic, and, I might add, entirely appealing compared with the fallen venereal desires of various sorts with which all men must or at least ought to contend in themselves. You can call the *hrossa* "heterosexual," but that usage is misleading since it suggests that human males whose venereal desires are focused on all attractive women are somehow more like the *hrossa* than are human males whose venereal desires are focused on all attractive men. Lewis nowhere suggests that prayer and the indwelling of the Holy Spirit will restore us fallen human males into a condition like that of the *hrossa* males.

Admittedly, some Christian men I've talked with are blessed with very quiescent, though still not unfallen, venereal drives—some toward men, others towards women. With less struggle than the rest of us, these men can direct their energy toward their prayer life in God and toward their interpersonal relationships—including, for those who are married, their friendship with their wife. It is a blessed state, but not something God bestows as a matter of course, no matter how much it may seem it would "make sense" for God to do—on grounds that we could organize our lives better, get more done for God and our fellow human beings, attain better focus on God during prayer, etc. In this area of human life as in others, what "makes sense" to human beings evidently doesn't always make sense to God. In any case, the Gospel does not teach that the Holy Spirit is in the business of producing "normal sexual personhood" in men, but seeks to redeem us into men of faith, hope, and love, who walk or at least limp in newness of life (Rom. 6:4).

So my certitude that God won't *heal* anyone into (fallen) heterosexuality is not based in modern psychology but in theology: given the wrongness of the adultery of the eyes (Matt. 5:28) that constitutes the desires of *heterosexual* men in the usual sense of the term, there's just no way that the Holy Spirit would *heal* anybody into such desires. Moreover, contrary to various still popular prejudices, "homosexual" men are the moral and spiritual equals of heterosexual men—neither worse nor better as regards courage, honesty, hard work, whatever. Yes, "God doesn't create homosexuals," but God doesn't create "heterosexuals" either—that is, lusters after all sexy women.

A grave confusion besets our understanding of these matters because of the various meanings given to "sexuality," "heterosexuality," "homosexuality," and "sexual orientation." None of these meanings is necessarily wrong, but serious harm and confusion result when a meaning of "sexuality" that's accurate in one context is introduced in a context where it cannot be accurate. For example, when "sexuality" means bringing together the sexes in life partnership and the procreation of children, then I agree that marriage is "sexual," and that all cultures have viewed marriage as "sexual." But I would also point out that all cultures until today have maintained that all men (including those today called "homosexual") are capable of the "sexuality" involved in marriage. Moreover, when "sexuality," "homosexuality" and "heterosexuality" refer to lust, then — as I've emphasized already — I doubt that marriage is very often "sexual." For "heterosexual" men, venery with the same woman soon becomes unexciting, though it may remain delightfully affectionate. For "homosexual" men, venery with a woman is rarely erotically exciting even at the beginning. So, considered as regards the duality of the sexes, marriage is "sexual" and "heterosexual." But considered as regards lust, marriage isn't "sexual" or "heterosexual."

Again, it isn't necessarily a mistaken usage when marriage between a man and a woman is described as "heterosexual marriage" in order to distinguish it from same-sex relationships. But if the understanding of "sexuality" as lust is brought in to that description so that "heterosexual" means lusting after all attractive women, then the use of "heterosexual" becomes misleading as a description for marriage, since the man may for whatever causes (for example, a current or former addiction to pornography, a homosexual "orientation," or a lack of much lust to begin with) may not lust after his wife, and venery between them is rare. The implication of "sexuality" as lust applied to marriage as "sexual" in the sense of uniting woman and man would be that marriages involving dwindling venereal desire are defective somehow, even though both spouses may find it a very satisfying life partnership and loving friendship. In this way, the prevailing usage of the terms "sexuality" and "heterosexuality" means that marriage is both sexual and unsexual, heterosexual and unheterosexual. And my basic objection to this incoherent usage is that it ends up denying "homosexual" men from the right to marry.

The varying meanings given to "sexuality" produce a similar confusion as regards therapies and ministries for "orientation change." In the usage that prevails in society generally, a "heterosexual" male is a guy whose sexual desires are "oriented" toward all attractive women. A "heterosexual" man must restrain, not express, his "sexuality" in order to marry and remain faithful to his wife. But in some secular and Christian therapies that seek to restore a homosexual man to "heterosexuality," "heterosexual" can mean a man who no longer has venery with other men and who seeks to find a woman to marry and raise a family with. His life "orientation" is changed less in the sense that his veneral desires become focused on all attractive women so that he must begin praying for self-restraint as regards sexy women, than in the sense that he orients his life toward loving his wife or fiancée and finding purpose in marriage and family. *This seems entirely right: a man's identity is constructed from the purposes he assigns for himself or accepts from God; a man's real orientation is his purposes in life.*

In this usage of "re-orientation," however, nothing is said about the focus of a man's venereal lust. As a man in such a program directs himself away from "homosexual behavior," he is said to be becoming "heterosexual." This would be okay if "heterosexual" were clearly meant to refer only to his growing understanding of and love for the complementarity of woman and man as partners in marriage and family. But since "heterosexual" in this sense is not clearly distinguished from "heterosexual" in the sense of lusting after sexy women, if the man still experiences strong desires toward venery with men, he is pushed back into fearing he's a fraud if he marries and raises a family with the woman he loves. In this way, he is pressured away from self-knowledge, since he thinks he can gain marriage and family only if he identifies himself as "heterosexual" in every sense. Even Davies and Rentzel, who are usually so common-sensical, use "sexuality" and "heterosexuality" in confusing ways. On the one hand, they teach that the created "sexual" duality and companionship of woman and man in Genesis concerns "heterosexuality." On the other hand, they uphold the Rousseauan thesis that human community is somehow derivative from venereal desires when they assert it is our "sexuality" that "draws us out of isolation"[4] — as though God's observation, "It is not good for the man to be alone," concerned the man's urges toward venereal release, not the man's need for a helper suitable to him (Gen 2:18-20).[5]

What is to be done with this contradictory use of "heterosexual," which causes so much pointless shame and suffering, and defines so many men as incapable of marriage? The general culture is not about to give up its definition of "heterosexuality" as lust toward all attractive women, or its definition of "orientation" as the focus of a man's lust either mostly on attractive men or mostly on attractive women. Hence, I recommend that Christian believers and other moral conservatives begin to specify what we mean more exactly; we should especially cease to use "heterosexuality" to mean the capacity to marry and raise a family, and we should remember that *"re-*

---

[4]Davies and Rentzel, 188, 67.

[5]Indeed, Genesis perhaps teaches that such desires, even of an unfallen sort, were not present before the human being ("Adam") was divided by God. It is not good for man to be alone not because the man has desires that he needs to discharge with another, but because he needs "a helper suitable for him" (Gen. 2:18). First the animals are presented as created for the sake of finding the man a suitable helper (2:19), but they are not adequate. Therefore, God makes the woman — not from the ground, but from the man himself. Hence he has his suitable helper, but also from this division he has the desire to cleave to her (Gen. 2:24), and, before the Fall, to her alone.

orientation" has less to do with venereal desire than with the changing of life purposes and learning the love and complementarity of man and woman as life partners. Perhaps, in many cases, along with the re-orientation in his self-understanding so that he now identifies himself as capable of a loving life partnership with a woman, there also occurs a change in the direction of a man's venereal desires. But changing the direction of his venereal desires isn't necessary in order for him to become a good and loving husband, and such change would bring with it new problems and challenges (how to deal with the sex appeal of all attractive women, not of his wife only).

Moreover, as regards life orientation, obviously there's no call in reason or in the Bible for Christian or secular therapies to seek to produce "heterosexuality" in the usual sense of the term. Most men who are "heterosexual" in this sense must restrain their sexual desires not merely for the sake of marriage and family, but even for the sake of having any way of life that transcends promiscuity, pornography, and prostitution. Yet many secular and Christian critics of "orientation change" therapies assert that these therapies never work because homosexual men aren't changed into heterosexuals (lusters after all attractive women). No matter how satisfying and purposeful a former homosexual's new life may be for him as a husband and father, if he isn't "turned on" by heterosexual pornography but presumably still would be by homosexual pornography,[6] critics insist that his healing and his new identity are bogus. But what really determines a

---

[6]Whether a man is turned on more by heterosexual pornography than by homosexual pornography is actually the criterion for love and meaning advocated by those who demand clinical "phallometric" testing to validate the results of orientation change programs.

man's "identity"? — what he finds purposeful in human relationships, or what he finds most venereally thrilling? If it's the latter, then I'm afraid every man who is "heterosexual" in the usual sense is "living a lie" if he confines his "sexuality" to a monogamous marriage with an aging wife.

But perhaps some readers suppose that "normal" heterosexuality (lust after all attractive women) is at least *intended* by secular and Christian orientation change therapies. For, humanly considered, probably what men and adolescents drawn toward venery with males want more than anything else is to be "normal" like (as they assume) "everybody else,"[7] no matter how many problems "normal" (hetero)sexuality causes "everybody else." It's entirely humanly comprehensible that people desire to be "normal" and to "fit in" with "everyone else." Yet I think Dr. Jeffrey Satinover puts the matter well when he says that a man who has been accustomed to having venery with men and who "enters the path to healing" comes to understand that "he is not defined by his sexual appetites." This man learns how to find in other men "a genuine, nonsexualized masculine comradeship and intimacy" and "how to relate aright to woman, as friend, lover, life's companion, and, God willing, mother of his children."[8] In common with others making similar arguments, "a homosexual" for Satinover is a man who is or recently has been having venery with men. This is not in itself an objectionable definition, but we should remember that the programs Satinover describes are not set up to change the "orientation" of married men who are aware of but not unduly troubled by their desires for venery with men.

---

[7]Mel White, 14.
[8]Satinover, 227.

Unfortunately, however, Satinover also refers to this "long and difficult" healing process as the "course to full restoration of heterosexuality" (227), even though this path doesn't involve any attempts to induce " full heterosexuality" in the usual sense. I don't say that "full heterosexuality" in the usual sense *never* results from the programs he describes, but it is evident that these programs do not intend to produce such heterosexualness. The programs and ministries that Satinover discusses focus on changing behavior and self-understanding. They seek to *restore* a man to an understanding of the complementarity of woman and man as loving friends and life partners together with God. Usually with this restoration, he can enjoy venery and intimate bodily affection with his wife, even though it rarely becomes as thrilling as venery with a variety of men.[9]

By "full heterosexuality," Satinover probably means much what Mary Stewart Van Leeuwen refers to as "heterosexual functioning."[10] For in these programs and therapies, the man wishing to be healed of homosexuality seeks to learn how to have sexual relations with his wife enough for them to bring children into the world. But he doesn't try to become "heterosexual" in the usual sense of the term — there's no reason to try to generate lust toward all attractive women! In fact, Satinover himself warns that the tendency toward "homosexual behavior" will remain: the desires "will not simply disappear, and later in times of great distress the old paths will beckon" (228). He rec-

---

[9]The nature of the heterosexuality that emerges from orientation-change therapies and ministries is well brought out by Davies and Rentzel, *Coming out of Homosexuality*, 27f, 145, 159, 162.

[10]Mary Stewart Van Leeuwen, *Gender and Grace: Love, Work and Parenting in a Changing World* (InterVarsity Press, 1990), 225.

ommends taking these "stirrings" as "a kind of storm warning, a signal that something is out of order" in a man's soul (228). But this is to say that in times of stress the former homosexual is not actually tempted to turn toward adulterous affairs, female prostitutes or heterosexual pornography — as are men who are "heterosexual" in the usual sense. I'm told that, unfortunately, many non-heterosexual men impel themselves into the drama of extramarital affairs, hiring prostitutes or even (heterosexual) sadomasochism in order to prove to themselves or to others that they really are *normal heterosexual men!*

Perhaps some men that pray for deliverance from homosexual desires are indeed healed by the Holy Spirit from lust altogether, or (more likely) are delivered from it into an inner shalom for a while. But when lust reappears, I'd say it is more likely to occur in the old direction (toward all attractive men) rather than in a new direction (toward all attractive women). For this reason I'd say that a man who intends to turn from "homosexual behavior" should learn to do this "one day at a time." This motto provided the breakthrough for recovering alcoholics: previously alcoholics were exhorted to "take the pledge" never to take another drink for the rest of their lives, but usually the prospect of day after day after day of refraining from drink was too great a burden to bear and they "fell off the [abstinence] wagon."

A bearable prospect was provided when Alcoholics Anonymous rediscovered the Gospel's focus on "the troubles of one day" (Matt. 6:34) and asking God for the grace to live one day at a time (Matt. 6:11). I might add that even living "one day at a time" must be taken to one day at a time: binding myself to an imagined whole future of more-or-less endless todays through which I must keep on living "one day at a time" is as overwhelming as any other more-or-less unending future that I could imagine for myself. Such imaginings are not at all the horizon of actually living this day in God's presence. I must never vow a life of living one day at a time, but only to try to live today one day at a time. I must not imagine even tomorrow as a today in its own right. I may count days of recovery only in retrospect.

Another tricky lesson is learning how to put together life plans of one sort or another—within the tentativeness and openness to revision that befits faith in God's providence—without falling away from living one day at a time. But however difficult it is to enter the narrow doorway into such existence, and although one finds how to enter usually only after several tries, living one day at a time is the best and freest way for anybody to live, and the only right way, the only possible way for a believer to live. But it is especially important for anybody struggling to break a strongly ingrained habit or addiction.

In sum, these programs and therapies attempt to enable a "homosexual" man to find a new orientation in his way of life and his understanding of God, himself, and others. They do not attempt to induce in him new lusts oriented toward all attractive women. Only a senseless man would "orient" his life purposes by the direction of his lusts.

But is it possible that men can change from lusters after attractive men into lusters after sexy women? In view of the enormous cross-cultural variations in human behavior and the surprising mixture of the changeable and unchangeable in the human soul, I'd say such changes do occur, but perhaps not frequently and probably not as a matter of course by this or that program or therapy. And we really shouldn't call the production of "heterosexuality" in the usual sense of the term a "healing" by Jesus Christ or the Holy Spirit! I should also emphasize that orientation-change therapy, which involves tremendous effort, isn't obligatory for all Christian men who experience strong venereal desires toward men. The scriptural and natural-law prohibitions against venery between men are satisifed by refraining from it. Many men who experience strong desires for such venery find their own ways to shrug off these urges, and choose — with varying degrees of difficulty — not to act upon them.

Chapter 19

But Marriage for *Homosexuals*?!?

I have spoken of the culturally entrenched belief that marriage is the expression of "heterosexuality." Because of this belief — which stems, I think, from the cultural impact of Rousseau — people today who try to bring healing to homosexual men wish to speak of this healing as a restoration of "heterosexuality." I'm sympathetic with this usage, especially since today's culture considers marriage an expression of "heterosexuality," and many men who experience strong desires for venery with men do wish to marry and have entirely valid reasons for marrying. For the same reason, these men will refuse to label themselves as "homosexual" or "gay"[1] (unless in the past tense as regards "homosexual behavior" or a "gay lifestyle" — as in the terms "former homosexual" or "exgay"). In a culture that perceives heterosexualness to be the only legitimate basis for marriage, such men will reject even the self-designation "non-heterosexual."

Anyone can understand the reluctance of men who marry despite venereal desires toward other men to refer to themselves even in their own minds as "gay" or "homosexual." But resisting self-knowledge has harmful con-

---

[1]Davies and Rentzel, 94-9, 177.

sequences, so these men should find some other way of remaining honest with themselves and with God (and I'd hope with a trustworthy pastor or other counselor) about these realities within themselves. Rather than bringing their self-identity into the issue, they might refer directly to "venereal desires toward men" in themselves. It should be possible for a man with strong venereal desires toward men to accept self-knowledge about these desire in a way that doesn't imply he is excluded from "normalness" or from marriage and raising a family.

Besides, as I have already emphasized, I think it makes no sense for anybody to identify and thus socially construct himself as a "sexual person" of one orientation or another. A man's choices, not his desires, define his personhood and moral and spiritual orientation. But in order not to be misunderstood, I wish to assert that I believe it's okay for a *homosexual* man to marry a woman with whom he can be a life partner and friend — and with whom to raise a family if that's in God's providence for them. There's no reason to suppose that a "homosexual" lacks what it takes to be a woman's friend and life partner. And the only way a "homosexual orientation" might detract from fatherhood is that a man may well become very depressed and beset by guilt and shame, and thus very remote from his children and their needs for parenting, if he believes his "sexual identity" makes his marriage invalid and his Christian faith a sham.

Of course, in defending the validity of marriage for "homosexuals," I do not have in mind men who are out having venery with men while also being married. That is as wrong as committing adultery with women.[2] When I

---

[2]However, I think gay liberationists make no sense when they maintain on the one hand that a "committed long-term" relationship between two gay men need not involve a promise of *Continued . . .*

argue that "homosexuals" may marry, I have in mind
men whose venereal desires remain entirely or mostly focused on men yet who have never become involved in venery with other men, or who have successfully settled (one
day at a time) into refraining from such venery. I agree
that a man who is habitually having venery with men
should not marry. "Homosexuality" in this sense must be
changed before a Christian man can rightly marry. But I
don't think a man lacks the capacity for marriage and
family life merely because his sexualness, if liberated,
would drive him toward venery with all attractive men,
rather than with all attractive women. Such a man has no
reason to fear that the love and meaning he and his wife
have in their marriage is actually bogus. And no one else
has any reason or any right to deem his marriage bogus
either.

I close with two quotations. The first, whose nonsensi-
cal conclusion is contradicted by its own first three sen-
tences, is from a present-day Christian spokesperson:

> You can genuinely love and respect a person. You
> can enjoy that person's company and celebrate
> that person's friendship. You can share that per-
> son's values and determine to be loyal and com-
> mitted to him or her for a lifetime. But when there
> is no sexual attraction, no erotic fascination, no po-
> tential for authentic physical passion, no sensual
> pull, no amorous play, no romantic component at
> the heart of it, there can be no intimacy, at least not

---

monogamy (sc. "forsaking all others") and on the other hand
insist that it is wrong for a man to be married to a woman yet
involve himself in venery with men outside the home. A "double life" of the one sort is surely as valid or invalid as a "double
life" of the other.

the kind of intimacy required to begin and to maintain a long-term, loving relationship, let alone a marriage.[3]

The second quotation is from perhaps the greatest human opponent of Christianity, yet to me it seems it speaks a truth we ought to embrace:

> Marriage as a long conversation. — When marrying you should ask yourself this question: do you believe you are going to enjoy talking with this woman into your old age? Everything else in a marriage is transitory, but most of the time that you're together will be devoted to conversation.[4]

---

[3]Mel White, 163.
[4] Nietzsche, *Human All Too Human* ¶406.

Postscript

*"What I Meant When I Said Non-Heterosexual
Men Are (Usually) Right When They Marry"*

**Jonathan Mills
(published in the Nov 18, 1997 edition of
Et Cetera, Regent College Student Newsletter)**

Shauna Stewart and the rest of the Regent Life Committee deserve a lot of credit and thanks for organizing the forum held last Thursday on issues relating to "homosexuality." Duffy Lott's chairpersonship gave us all a reasonable, calm and polite discussion of a variety of opinions on these issues, and these issues are probably the most controversial that there are today!

Obviously a single forum can't begin to settle things, and I hope that last Thursday marked only the beginning of further discussions on what "human sexuality" is and means — if indeed "sexuality" is turning out to be a helpful term for human self-understanding at all! But I would like that chance to try to clarify one thing, because many people afterward showed concern that a Regent lecturer would propose that it is OK for "homosexual" men to marry each other. But what I meant is that it is OK for a non-heterosexual man to marry a woman. That opinion may also seem offensive, but it is certainly congruent with Scripture and church tradition. Only with the emergence of the notion of "sexuality" this century has it come to be assumed that some people are excluded from marriage because their "orientation." All cultures except our own suppose that marriage and family is the way most men should live their lives. Whether it is OK for a married man to have sex outside marriage with unattached women or with men has always been treated separately from the meaningfulness of marriage for him, whether for him sex with men or sex with women would be more thrilling.

The basic point I wanted to make was pastoral—in my opinion we have to understand how likely it is that most men with "these desires" are going to override today's prohibition of marriage to them. Marriage and family is still the thing going on in our society. It is difficult especially for men to feel they belong without being married to a woman. Even aside from the high purposes and belongingness of Christian marriage, it's humanly understandable that people want to "fit in" and feel "normal"; and most men feel they will be part of human society only if they are married. I'm not saying there's anything wrong with being single or that churches shouldn't do a lot more to recognize what single people have to offer the Kingdom of God. But surely we should face the fact that a lot of guys are going to want to marry the woman they love and to raise a family with her even if their primary "sexual orientation" is toward men.

So I think we can't expect that most men and adolescents will tell their pastors or other counselors that "these desires" are going on in them, because they know that our culture assumes the presence of "these desires" excludes them from marriage and family—and from normalness and fitting in. They don't want to go off into whatever "gay sexuality" is doing at the moment.

As for "orientation change" ministries, most nonhetero guys hesitate to enter these programs because they fear that if they do not emerge from the process as a heterosexual (and this is by no means a guarantee, and there is some ambiguity as to what "heterosexual" means as the goal of an orientation change process anyway), they'll lose their right to anything but celibacy (if they remain an orthodox Christian) or a gay lifestyle. In my opinion, today most "non-hetero" men are still marrying and raising families — the way such men have always done. But today's belief that marriage is an "expression" of "sexuality" binds upon these men tremendous burdens of shame and fear of discovery.

Bibliography

Aquinas, Thomas. *Summa theologica* 2-2 qq 151-56.

Aristotle. *Nicomachean Ethics.*

_____. *Politics.*

Arnold, Johann Christoph. *A Plea for Purity: Sex Marriage & God.* Plough, 1996.

Augustine, *Confessions.*

Bataille, Georges. *Eroticism: Death & Sensuality*; trans., Mary Dalwood. City Lights Books, 1986.

Barth, Karl. *Protestant Thought: From Rousseau to Ritschl*; trans., Brian Cozens. Ayer Company, 1959.

Bloom, Allan. *The Closing of the American Mind.* Simon & Schuster, 1987.

_____. *Love and Friendship.* Simon & Schuster, 1993.

Bockmuehl, Klaus. *The Unreal God of Modern Theology.* Helmers & Howard, 1988.

Boswell, John. *Christianity, Social Tolerance, and Homosexuality: Gay People in Western Europe from the Beginning of the Christian Era to the Fourteenth Century.* University of Chicago, 1980.

Burns, David D. *Feeling Good: The New Mood Therapy.* New American Library, 1980.

Clark, Mary Franzen, and Mary Elizabeth McKheen, "When Gay Christian Men Marry Straight Christian Women," *Journal of Psychology and Christianity* 13:3 (1994) 255-63.

Congregation for the Doctrine of the Faith, "Letter to the Bishops of the Catholic Church on the Pastoral Care of Homosexual Persons" (10 Nov., 1986).

Catechism of the Catholic Church. Canadian Conference of Catholic Bishops, 1994.

Cooper, Barry. *Michel Foucault: An Introduction to the Study of His Thought.* Edwin Mellen Press, 1981.

Crawford, David. *Easing the Ache: Gay Men Recovering From Compulsive Behaviors.* Dutton, 1990.

Davies, Bob, and Lori Rentzel. *Coming out of Homosexuality: New Freedom for Men and Women.* InterVarsity Press, 1993.

Denneny, Michael, "Gay Manifesto for the 80's," *Christopher Street* (Jan., 1981) 13-21.

Dinter, Paul. "Disabled for the Kingdom: Celibacy, Scripture and Tradition," *Commonweal* (Oct. 12, 1990), 571-76.

Eribon, Didier. *Michel Foucault;* trans., Betsy Wing. Harvard University Press, 1991.

Foucault, Michel. *The History of Sexuality, Volume 1: An Introduction;* trans., Robert Hurley. Random House, 1980.

_____. *The Order of Things: An Archeology of the Human Sciences.* Random House, 1994.

Gilder, George. *Sexual Suicide.* Quadrangle, 1972.

_____. *Wealth and Poverty.* Basic Books, 1981.

Goss, Robert. *Jesus Acted Up: A Gay and Lesbian Manifesto.* Harper Collins, 1993.

Greeley, Andrew. *Faithful Attraction: Discovering Intimacy, Love, and Fidelity in American Marriage.* Tom Doherty, 1991.

Grenz, Stanley. *Sexual Ethics: A Biblical Perspective.* Word Publishing, 1990.

Hegel, GWF. *Philosophy of Right;* trans., T.M. Knox. Oxford University Press, 1967.

Heidegger, Martin. *An Introduction to Metphysics;* trans., Ralph Manheim. Yale University Press, 1986.

Hickling, Meg. *Speaking of Sex: Are You Ready to Answer the Questions Your Kids Will Ask?* Northstone, 1996.

Johnson, Fenton. "Wedded to an Illusion: Do Gays and Lesbians Really Want the Right to Marry?" *Harper's* (Nov. 1996), 43-50.

Johnson, Paul. *Intellectuals.* Weidenfeld & Nicolson, 1988.

Kant, Immanuel. *Kant on History;* ed., Lewis White Beck. Bobbs-Merrill, 1963

_____. *Kant's Political Writings;* ed., Hans Reiss; trans., H.B. Nisbet. Cambridge University Press, 1977.

Lewis, C.S. *The Abolition of Man.* Macmillan, 1965.

_____. *The Four Loves.* Collins, 1963.

_____. *Mere Christianity.* Collins, 1955.

_____. *Out of the Silent Planet.* Pan Books, 1952.

_____. *The Screwtape Letters.* Collins, 1955.

_____. *The Weight of Glory and other addresses.* Eerdmans, 1965.

Löwith, Karl. *From Hegel to Nietzsche: The Revolution in Nineteenth-Century Thought;* trans., David E. Green. Columbia University Press, 1964.

Macey, David. *The Lives of Michel Foucault.* Hutchinson, 1990.

Marx, Karl. *The Marx-Engels Reader,* second edition; ed., Robert Tucker. W.W. Norton, 1978.

Masters, William H. et al, *Heterosexuality.* Harper Collins, 1994.

Mills, Jonathan. "John Boswell's Corruption of the Greeks." (A review of John Boswell's *Christianity, Social Tolerance and Homosexuality*) *Crux* 18:3 (1982) 21-27.

_____. "Tootsie: A Review Article" *Crux* 19:3 (1983) 8-14.

_____. "Phylogyny Recapitulates Androgyny: Or the Attempt to Get 'Beyond Man and Woman'." *The Hillsdale Review* 6:4 (1985), 24-35.

_____. "Morally Dionysian Religious Authority vs. The Rules," *Crux* 33:1 (1997) 22-30.

Nietzsche, Friedrich. *Dawn of Morning* ("Daybreak").

_____. *Human, All Too Human.*

_____. *Mixed Opinions and Maxims.*

———. *Schopenhauer as Educator.*

———. *Twilight of the Idols.*

———. *The Will to Power.*

Payne, Leanne. *The Broken Image: Restoring Personal Wholeness Through Healing Prayer.* Crossway Books, 1981.

Perry, Troy. *Don't Be Afraid Anymore: The Story of Reverend Troy Perry and the Metropolitan Community Churches,* with Thomas L.P. Swicegood. St. Martin's Press, 1990.

———. *The Lord is My Shepherd and He Knows I'm Gay,* as told to Charles L. Lucas. Bantam Books, 1972, 1978.

Plato. *Charmides.*

———. *Symposium.*

———. *Phaedrus.*

———. *The Laws.*

Ratzinger, Joseph Cardinal. *The Ratzinger Report: An Exclusive Interview on the State of the Church*; ed. Vittorio Messori; trans., Salvator Attanasio, Graham Harrison. Ignatius Press, 1985.

Rousseau, Jean-Jacques. *Discourse on the Origin and the Foundations of Inequality Among Men* ("Second Discourse").

———. *Discourse on the Sciences and the Arts* ("First Discourse").

———. *Emile.*

———. *On the Social Contract.*

———. *Politics and the Arts: Letter on the Theatre.*

Satinover, Jeffrey. *Homosexuality and the Politics of Truth.* Baker Books, 1996.

Schmidt, Thomas E.. *Straight and Narrow? Compassion and Clarity in the Homosexuality Debate.* InterVarsity, 1995.

Shilts, Randy. *And the Band Played On: Politics, People, and the AIDS Epidemic.* St. Martin's Press, 1987.

Smedes, Lewis B. *Sex For Christians.* Eerdmans, 1976.

Stackhouse, Max L. *Covenant and Commitments: Faith, Family and Economic Life.* Westminster John Knox Press, 1997.

Tannahill, Reay. *Sex in History.* Stein and Day, 1982.

Van Leeuwen, Mary Stewart. *Gender and Grace: Love, Work and Parenting in a Changing World.* InterVarstity Press, 1990.

Weber, Max. *From Max Weber: Essays In Sociology;* ed., and trans., H.H. Gerth, C. Wright Mills. Oxford University Press, 1946.

White, Mel. *Stranger at the Gate.* Simon & Schuster, 1994.

Whitehead, Barbara Dafoe. "The Failure of Sex Education," *The Atlantic Monthly* (Oct., 1994), 55-80.

Williams, Robert. *Just as I Am: A Practical Guide to Being Out, Proud and Christian.* HarperCollins, 1992.

Wojtyla, Karol. *The Splendor of Truth.* Éditiones Paulines, 1993.

Printed in the United States
23838LVS00001B/350

9 781573 830911